KT-143-705

THE MAGIC OF THINKING $UCCE$$

our Personal Guide to Financial Independence

by Dr. David J. Schwartz, author of

THE MAGIC OF THINKING BIG

Foreword by Melvin Powers

Melvin Powers
Wilshire Book Company
12015 Sherman Road
North Hollywood, California 91605

Copyright 1987 by David J. Schwartz, Ph.D.
All Rights Reserved

Library of Congress Catalog Card Number: 86-51563
ISBN 0-87980-420-3
Printed in the United States of America

For Sara Ann Schwartz

An extra-special BIG THINKER! Keep showing all of us how we can
- Love by sharing love,
- Find happiness in simple things,
- Prosper by giving our talents.

To you, Sara, a wonderful granddaughter, friend, and special buddy, and to your sister, Abigail Amanda, and to your brother, David James, this book is dedicated.

Foreword

What is the most valuable sense that we as human beings possess? Is it our ability to see the panorama of life around us, to hear the sounds of song and speech, to feel the pleasures of the physical world? Or is it, perhaps, the ability to taste and to smell the sweetness and richness of nature's bounty?

Dr. David Schwartz believes our most precious sense is "mindsight" — the capacity to envision our life in its most satisfying form. But mindsight is much more than just mentally seeing our life at its best. It is an attitude and a plan of action; it is a dream and the ability to make that dream come true.

Packed with practical tools and emotional support, *The Magic of Thinking Success* helps us to discover and to put to effective use this powerful "sixth sense" we all possess. Few of us even know what we want, much less have a plan to get it. Yet, without such direction, our lives are less exciting, less fulfilling, and less successful than they could be. This book tells us how to get ourselves onto the path that will bring happiness and satisfaction, and gives us valuable techniques to help us stay on it. It is a step-by-step guide to achieving personal success.

Personal success, says Dr. Schwartz, is synonymous with personal happiness. How you feel about yourself, your job, your relationships, and the world contributes to or detracts from your personal success.

The author describes truly successful people as being those who greet each new day with enthusiasm, confidence, and optimism. They feel good about themselves and about the life they have chosen to lead. They know that to *have* it all *in* life, they have to *give* their all *to* life. They "love love and love work." These individuals are adept at motivating others and derive great pleasure from sharing in the joy of their achievements. They are caring and responsive to others, treat them well and are treated well in return. Through mindsight, they know that work, challenge, and even sacrifice are all parts of life, and they routinely turn adversities into opportunities for personal growth. Successful people conquer fear by facing it and overcome pain by experiencing it. They have the knack of creating happiness in their everyday lives that also is uplifting to those fortunate enough to be around them. Their usual smile is evidence of their inner strength and positive approach to living.

Do you consider yourself to be one of those who have attained personal success? Are you as happy as you want to be? Are you living your dream life, or settling for what you think is all you can have? Does every day seem like a wonderful opportunity for beautiful, gratifying experiences? If not, Dr. Schwartz has an important message for you: No one has to settle for less than a full, rich, rewarding life. He identifies the essential attitudes and actions and clearly outlines the steps necessary to becoming personally successful.

Whether or not you will ever be able to live the life you have wished for is now entirely up to you. You can make your dream life become a reality by applying the knowledge contained within these pages.

Melvin Powers
Publisher, Wilshire Book Company

Preface

Here is an amazing fact: One family in every 100 has a net worth of $1 million or more. Today there are almost a million millionaires!

Meanwhile, countless people in less-than-wealthy circumstances ask, "What must I do to acquire more money and enjoy the life style that comes with it? How can I achieve greater happiness, prosperity, and satisfaction in my life?"

The Magic of Thinking Success has a key purpose: To help you, regardless of your age, sex, education, family, background, health, or occupation, make the transition from where you are to where you want to be.

Consider this: Eighty percent of today's millionaires "made it" in the last 20 years. And they are wealthy in non-monetary ways, too. Most of today's financially successful people enjoy hard work, place top emphasis on their families, and are well respected.

How are today's achievers becoming wealthy? Most reach financial independence in their own businesses. A large share (20 percent) become millionaires through network marketing.

Humility is a characteristic of the new wealthy. My friend, Dr. Thomas Stanley, the number one expert on millionaires, reports that 15,000 of them live in mobile homes! And more drive pickup trucks than drive expensive European imports.

Fortunes are made in people's minds. Your mind is the ultimate personal computer. And you are its programmer. You can instruct your mind computer to select the right job opportunity, to make the right investment, or to choose the right mate. You can program your mind to deal effectively with people, to exercise influence, and to acquire wealth.

You see, over a time each of us becomes exactly what we program our minds to be. A prosperous person programs prosperous thinking into his or her mind. And a miserable human being instructs his or her mind to "make me unhappy, mediocre, boring, and average."

In a nutshell, your mind, as with any computer, is your obedient servant, ready to do precisely what you tell it. Remember, too, your mind doesn't care what instructions you give it. It always obeys. Program it with reasons why you will succeed and you will enjoy success. But tell your computer, "I am a failure," and, obediently, your mind, processing the program you gave it, will prove you are, indeed, a loser.

Your mind is like soil in a garden. The soil doesn't care what seeds you plant — crabgrass or melons, weeds or cabbage. The soil (your mind) nourishes what you plant. Plant prosperity seeds and reap prosperity; plant poverty seeds and harvest poverty.

Often, successful people say to me, "Five years ago *I just knew* I was going to make it in my own business," or "I *made up my mind* I wouldn't give up or take no for an answer," and "Once I became *committed,* something inside me just wouldn't let go."

These comments indicate minds that are programmed to win.

I've heard other people say, "I knew I couldn't make it in that job," "I felt whipped before I even started," and "I've always been a loser and this experience just proved it."

These comments describe people who programmed their minds to fail.

Learning the skills of successful mind programming is important to your success. Benefit by knowing how to influence others, how to project a more valuable you, how to achieve big, worthwhile goals. Capitalize on your strengths. Destroy "I'm-only-average" thought patterns. Reach above mediocrity, dullness, and apathy. Conquer the real cause of stress, worry, and fear.

Remember, you have the power to be what you want, go where you choose, accomplish great objectives, climb any ladder. You can grow a great life with positive mind programming.

Sound simplistic? I hope so! The laws of success are simple The "how" of success is so simple, so common, that most people, expecting something complicated and difficult, fail to discover the road to influence, power, wealth, and plain good living.

The winners in today's economic contest don't just see an opportunity — they *seize* it. To them, a setback means "to bounce back." It never means "to quit." People who make success a habit view work as a stimulating challenge, not as a sentence in a company prison.

Know the 20/80 law. It says 80 percent or more of everything worthwhile is owned, achieved, or created by 20 percent or less of the people. Know the law because it applies in every aspect of life.

Imagine a reunion 10 years from now of 20 people you know. Assume that 100 apples is the total net worth of the group of 20. Here is how the apples will be divided: Sixteen of the people — the mediocrities — will share only 20 apples. But the four succeeders will have 80 apples or 20 each — 20 apples for each succeeder; only a little more than one apple for each mediocrity.

One hundred and forty years ago, John Greenleaf Whittier wrote these thought-provoking lines:

"For all sad words of tongue or pen
The saddest are these: 'It might have been!' "

It is sad for anyone, whether they are aged 20, 40, or 80, to look backward in time and to regret. It is enormously disillusioning to live in a world where ordinary people are becoming millionaires and you are not. It hurts to see a person with less ability and education than you have win promotions and become your boss. It is disappointing to have turned down an opportunity and then see another seize the same opportunity and make millions from it. It is painful beyond description not to be able to give your children the start they need in life. And it cripples your spirit to feel enslaved when others live free, exciting, challenging lives.

Now, here is good news. Life can be a series of victories, not disappointments. No one is condemned to endure the agony of Whittier's words "It might have been." This book shows you how to live life successfully, joyfully, and abundantly. Read it, study it, and practice its philosophy so you can rewrite the gloom Whittier described:

"For all *happy* words we speak or write
The happiest are these: 'I won the fight!' "

Table of Contents

Chapter 1

The Successful Life Begins With a Dream

Successful people do not look at their families, their jobs, their health, or their net worth as they are. They jump ahead of the masses and do one simple but profound thing: They look at life as it can be, not as it is. They perceive life as it will be after application of their persistent, intelligent, "I-will-win" efforts.

Progress in any activity is made only when its potentiality is envisioned, not when it is restricted by reality. Great architects, construction people, and investors don't see the reality of big city slums and worn-out buildings. They see potential possibilities in converting slums into new communities where people can live, work, and play. Every business, school, institution, and building is a dream someone made happen.

A great life always begins with a great dream.

Each human being has two kinds of vision: Eyesight and mindsight. Eyesight tells us what objects are around us. Eyesight forms pictures of trees, people, buildings, mountains, water, stars, and other physical, tangible things. Eyesight is physical.

Mindsight is different from eyesight. Mindsight is the power to see not what is but what can be when human intelligence is applied. Mindsight is the power to dream. Mindsight forms pictures of the future — the home we want, the family relationship we desire, the income we will enjoy, vacations we want to take, or our wealth at some point in time.

Eyesight is strictly physical and sees only reality. Mindsight is purely spiritual and sees only potentiality. Mindsight reveals what is not yet real nor tangible. How we choose to use our mindsight to dream determines our success (achievement, influence, and satisfaction), our wealth (income, net worth, and physical well-being), and our happiness (respect, joy, and contentment).

People differ little in eyesight. At a very early age, all children using eyesight can clearly distinguish objects, such as people, buildings, stars, and water. But people differ enormously in mindsight or mental images of what is not yet real nor tangible. A great majority of people "see" the future as filled with trouble. In the work department, they "see" spending a life in a mediocre, modest-paying job. In the social department, their mindsight "sees" little joy but lots of boredom and big problems. And in the home department, they "see," at best, only an ordinary, dull, problem-plagued existence.

On the other hand, a few success-directed dreamers see the future as filled with challenge. They see work as a road to advancement and prestige, and to large rewards. Creative dreamers see social relationships as encouraging, as stimulating, and as fun. In their home department, they see excitement, adventure, and happiness. They choose to dream of a good and great life.

Whether we spend life winning or losing depends on how we use our mindsight — what we choose to "see" or to dream. Each of us has the power to make this life a heaven or a hell, depending on how we choose to dream about it. Those who see life as a heaven are the winners; those who view life as a hell are the losers.

Some believe luck or chance determine their destiny. These people think that fortunes, success, and the good life depend on the roll of the dice, on the spin of a wheel, or on a randomly selected number in a state lottery.

How foolish.

The statistical odds of winning a million dollars in a lottery are many millions to one. Lotteries appeal to people who believe wealth can be had with an investment of only a few dollars. The target market for lotteries or any kind of gambling are people who think they can acquire wealth by chance or luck.

Wishing is different from dreaming. Wishing is passive and inactive. Wishing is an idle pastime with no brains or effort behind it. But dreaming is backed up with an action plan to produce results.

Jim "wishes" he would be promoted. But Jim never volunteers to do extra work, he avoids helping co-workers who need help, and he never submits an idea, asking, "Why don't we try this?" Will Jim's wish for more money come true? Of course not.

Mary "wishes" she could become a partner in the accounting firm where she works. But Mary "doesn't have time" to take advanced accounting courses in school, nor does she volunteer to help out when 12- and 14-hour days are needed. And Mary does not go out of her way to pass on tax-saving ideas to clients. Result? Mary's wish is wasted.

Tim and Susan "wish" they could have their own successful business. But Tim and Susan place weekend recreation first. Something — parties, trips, entertainment — always exhausts their time. And their wish remains only a wish.

You see, anyone can wish. But a dreamer takes action on what he or she wants.

You can divide the people you know into two categories: The winners and the losers. Winners are active dreamers working to convert their dreams into positive, tangible accomplishments. Losers are inactive faultfinders who believe the "system" is against them and luck or fate determines what will happen.

Losers are cynical. "June got her promotion because of her 'extra curriculars' with the boss." "Fred got the big order because he bribed the buyer." "Pete and Sara have a new Mercedes, but they probably had to finance it for five years."

Winners are people of good will. "I'm glad for John. He worked hard and deserves his reward." "Betty's promotion proves there is reward when you give the job your best."

Losers are pessimists. "The economy is bankrupt. The national debt and the trade imbalance are certain to create the worst depression ever, so don't bother to invest for the future."

People who dream big think, "Regardless of how good or bad the economy is now, it will get even better. It always does. I'm banking on a great future. Besides, I can't control what happens to the nation's economy, but I can control *my* economy."

Losers are selfish. "That's not my job. Why should I help her?" "Nobody ever did anything for me. So, I'm not going to do anything for other people."

Winners are generous. "The more I help other people make money, the more money I'll make in return." "Good deeds for other people are always rewarded."

Losers want something for nothing. "I work for a big company. It can afford to pay me more money." "I've been here ten years. The company ought to pay me more." "Cheat on the expense account. Everybody else does." "I'm going to take three days sick leave even though I'm not sick. It's my 'right.'"

Winners know "There is no free lunch," "Sacrifice means investing for my future and those I love," and "Hard work makes happy people."

A great reward in life is helping other people maximize their potential. Managers tell me, "I take enormous satisfaction in recovering people from mediocrity and pointing them toward success." Salespeople relate how they help a customer turn a business around and make it profitable. Coaches describe how they give courage and direction to an athlete and then watch him become famous.

I recently attended a banquet for a fifth-grade school teacher. It is unusual for adults to care about or even remember their fifth-grade teacher. But hundreds of people attended and expressed their appreciation to Ms. Bower for what she had done for them.

After the reception, I asked her, "What did you do for the kids?"

Carefully, she explained, "I never looked at the children as children. I trained my mind to see them as people on a journey to adulthood, as young trees growing slowly but surely into giant oaks. I saw my educational responsibilities in three dimensions: Help them to become good parents, good citizens, and good workers. That key thought," she went on, "gave me guidance in how I taught and what I taught."

What a wonderful example! It is far superior to simply looking at the children and thinking that teaching is only a job. Ms. Bower saw the potential in the kids and her responsibility to give direction to that potential.

HOW TO GROW A DREAM

It's easy to dismiss someone else's achievements with he or she "was lucky," "had superior athletic ability," "was born a genius," "got in on the ground floor," or, in some way, lucked into success.

But success, wealth, and happiness do not come from luck. All accomplishments stem from dreams courageous people convert into reality. The great structures we work in, the agricultural enterprises that feed us, the industries that entertain us, the institutions that educate and inspire evolved from the ideas and dreams of productive individuals.

When you see a successful business, school, entertainment, or political institution, you are looking at an individual's dream grown into reality. A happy family is made possible through creative dreaming

Think of life as a garden.

At one time, the great valleys of California were deserts. But some people with dreams saw the "useless" land as irrigated areas used to grow food people need. Acting on their dreams, many who bought this land became wealthy.

Successful people are individuals who convert their dreams into services and products other people desire.

Growing a dream into success is like growing a garden. Six steps are involved:

1. Select your dream seed.
2. Prepare your mind to accept the seed.
3. Plant your dream seed.
4. Nourish your dream.
5. Focus your energy. Put "I will' to work.
6. Hire time to work for you.

STEP I:
SELECT YOUR DREAM SEED

Just as careful selection of corn seed is important to good farming, wise choice of dream seed is essential for good living.

Seeds always grow their own kind. Wheat seeds always grow wheat, never corn. Lemon seeds always grow lemon trees, never peach trees.

A dream seed also grows its own kind. Two key questions in deciding what dream seed to plant are, "What do I want to do?" and "What is the profit potential of the dream?"

WHAT WILL MY DREAM PRODUCE?
WHAT IS ITS PROFIT POTENTIAL?

Profit is your reward for serving others. In business, profit is what we earn from offering good products and services at a fair price.

In non-businesses, such as schools and civic organizations, profit may be the number of people we help to learn and to live better. Profit to a church may be the number of people helped; to a charity, profit may be the number of meals served to indigent people; and to a trade association, profit may be its service to members. Always, profit represents the good we do.

Regardless of your dream, you want to harvest the maximum profit because profit is the way results are measured.

Potential counts big. Each person has several talents. A key to the good life is selecting and developing one's best talent. A path to a sad life is doing something we know is wrong. An artist may receive $25 for a painting and be happy beyond description because she knows her effort is good for the soul of another.

As you select a dream, ask "How much satisfaction will implementation of my dream give others?"

Remember, there is nothing right or wrong with money. Money is simply (a) a tool we use to energize and direct human activity, and (b) a device for keeping score. On one hand, money builds and operates schools and hospitals and runs our government. On the other hand, money finances crime, bribes those in trusted positions, and corrupts some people in government, in education, and in the church.

WHAT DO I WANT TO DO?

Success would be simple if we could go to a store and tell the merchant, "Sell me a dream seed that is guaranteed to make me happy and wealthy." But we can't. Dream seeds are not for sale. Nor can they be inherited, borrowed, or otherwise transferred. Friends, parents, and teachers may suggest goals, but only you can answer, "What dream is best for me?"

Often I'm asked, "Where (what occupation) can I make a lot of money?" In a way, that question is like asking on a bright day, "Where is the sunlight?" or, asking aboard a ship on the ocean, "Where is the water?"

The answer to "Where is the money?" is: "Everywhere." Jobs in the United States have great economic potential. Most musicians earn small incomes. But a few earn millions every year. Typically, ministers are poorly paid. But some are richly rewarded financially. Many small-business owners earn little. But some prosper and reap fantastic rewards.

In terms of economic opportunity, it is not the occupation that makes a person prosper. It is the person who makes the person prosper.

The best dream seed is the one you can't get out of your mind — an idea that never leaves you, a cause or a purpose that absorbs you, an obsession. That one thing you *must* do is your ideal dream seed.

STEP II:
PREPARE YOUR MIND TO ACCEPT THE SEED

Gardeners know that the better the soil is prepared before they plant, the better the seeds will grow. The mind is to your dream what soil is to a plant. The better your mind is prepared to accept your dream seed, the more certain your dream will develop good roots. The well-prepared soil says, "I accept the seed." The mind ready for a dream says, "I accept the dream. I'm ready for it."

Take pride in your dream machine. Your mind, the place where you will plant and grow your dream, is unique. In all creation there is no one who looks, talks, walks, and thinks like you.

Be glad of it. Being unique means you have the best dream machine there is for the dream you want to make happen.

Some people say, "I wish I could trade places with (the boss, a wealthy person, a brother or sister, someone in great power like the President of the United States)." People who say this overlook the greatest gift of all — uniqueness.

You might want to trade jobs with the President of the United States. But you certainly wouldn't want to change lives. It is healthy to like your life. For your purposes, you have the best dream machine there is.

Wash your mind with Solution PMA. Your hands and face get dirty with dust, grime, and grease. In time, your mind can get dirty with discouragement, defeat, and disappointment. Just as we need to wash our hands before eating, we need to wash our minds before tackling a dream.

To give your dream strong roots, you must wash away memories that hold you back — as the time you may have attempted an endeavor that failed, making you look foolish and feel humiliated, or you may have suffered defeat in business, marriage, or investments.

To cleanse your brain, spray it with "Solution PMA" — positive-mental-attitude thoughts about your successes and accomplishments, praise you received from people you respect, or victories you achieved.

Look at a setback only to learn a lesson. Then refuse to relive it. Wash away negative memories. Plant your dream in a disinfected seedbed.

Develop your dream trip brochure. Imagine a friend suggesting the two of you take a trip to Moscow. But you have no interest in going. No reason in particular. You just don't want to go. Then your friend shows you pictures of some of the history, culture, customs, entertainment, and social problems that make up Moscow, and soon you are ready to go!

The more we know about anything, the more curious we become. Our minds accept our dreams the same way. The clearer the image you have of your dream, the more enthusiastic about it you become.

Part of preparing your mind to accept your dream is seeing it with your physical vision as clearly as possible.

Dreaming of an extra special home? Visit the neighborhood often and look at your dream house.

Dreaming of a great education for your children? Visit the university where your dream will happen.

Dreaming of a new career or a business of your own? Read all you can about it. Talk to people in the career or business. Put your plan on paper — the broad picture first, followed by the details.

Use your mental vision to prepare your brain to grow a great dream.

STEP III:
PLANT YOUR DREAM SEED

Think of a carefully selected extra-special tomato seed. Potentially, that little seed can grow 25 pounds of wonderful fruit. One seed will easily produce one million times its weight in good food. But the seed with all its promise won't grow any tomatoes unless it is planted.

So it is with great dreams. The best ideas in the world for making money, building a business, solving a social problem, or making an improvement in life are useless until they are planted. And when great ideas are planted in a well-prepared mind, tremendous results happen. Every great enterprise from McDonald's to Ford to Hershey's candy to Coca-Cola was once simply an idea *that was planted.*

A fortune is an idea acted upon.

All around us are people who let the "I-wish-I-had-but-didn't" disease beat them. This ailment takes on many forms. In speaking about investments, people say, "I wish I had bought XYZ stock ten years ago," or "My sixth sense told me to invest in ABC but I didn't."

In talking about going into business, people who didn't plant their dream say, "I wanted to start a business back in 1980 but I had some problems," or "Looking back, I could kick myself for passing up the ABC opportunity."

In discussing careers, you'll often hear people describe how they let dream opportunities die with "I wanted to go into business for myself, but I never could see my way clear," or "Way back, I really wanted to get into computers, but I thought they were only a fad."

The "I-wish-I-had-but-didn't" disease is as common as the cold. That fact, coupled with the wisdom in the old saying "The saddest words of tongue or pen are 'it might have been,' " make life disappointing for people with great ideas who let them die.

Here are two plans for putting dreams to work:

1. *Plant the dream.* Take action. Start now. Today I received a phone call from a car dealer asking me to speak to his sales staff to celebrate their best year. He told me, "Eight years ago I was a police officer. The job was OK, but the low pay, politics, and negative environment were getting to me. One weekend I read your book *The Magic of Thinking Big* and noticed a quote in Chapter 10, 'Get the action habit.' Monday morning I reported to the chief and resigned. I decided if I were going to enjoy this life, I had to start now. So I did. And in only eight years, I'm financially independent."

That's what happens when we act to make dreams come true.

Want to go to school and earn a degree? *Start now.* Feel you're not moving ahead in your job? *Talk to your superior now.* Deep in debt? *Rearrange your finances now.*

2. *Don't wait for perfect conditions to plant your dream.* As a kid on the farm, I learned early that planting conditions are never perfect. It was always a little too wet or a little too dry to plant a crop. Or it might have been a little too early or a bit too late. One spring, I remember my father saying, "We've never planted corn this late before and we may not get much of a crop. But if we don't plant now, we won't get any crop at all."

So, watch those "after" escape clauses as "I'll take action on my dream after the economy improves," or "... after I'm out of debt," or "... after the holidays," or "... after so and so does such and such."

Remember, in the long run you'll be ahead!

STEP IV:
NOURISH YOUR DREAM SEED

Think some more about your tomato seed. It is an excellent seed, the soil is well prepared, and you have planted it. But to grow and pay off with good-tasting tomatoes, the seed needs nourishment — sunlight, fertilizers, and water.

Your dream seed also requires nutrition — imagination, encouragement, and ideas — to grow and make you prosper. According to government figures, an incredible two million businesses are started each year but only a small fraction succeed. In one way or another, neglect is the main reason.

Let me tell you about a couple, Tom and Susan, who are making their dream of financial independence and prosperity grow in a multi-level marketing business.

Susan explained it this way:

"We decided that the basic idea — the dream seed as you call it — had all the potential we needed. We had seen other people make it work — people who weren't any smarter or better than we were. So, we decided — no, we made a *commitment* — to make our business work. We set aside three hours every week night and eight hours every weekend. To find the time, we had to make 'sacrifices.' " She laughed, "We gave up TV, bowling — things we didn't enjoy, anyway.

"We met with people in the business at least once a week in person and talked to our group leader as often as needed by phone. We got lots of ideas from people who were doing well in the business. When we faced a problem, we'd call for help. And this gave us some of the sunlight and encouragement we needed.

"We used every minute of our spare time to make the business grow. We attended meetings, seminars, and we fed our business just as carefully as we feed our two kids."

Tom told me that in their first year in business they netted $31,000. But the key point is they are making their business work by caring for it, feeding it so it will succeed.

The point: Once the dream is planted, feed it. Attend seminars. Go to school if necessary. Join trade associations. Talk to successful people. Read.

Let other success-minded people help you. There is an old law of human nature — "Birds of a feather flock together." That rule will always stand. So, if you want to make a large income and accumulate wealth, affiliate with people who are comfortable earning large incomes and who are determined to acquire even more net worth. You become like the people you associate with every day. If your circle of friends is people who are resigned to mediocrity and the "whatever-will-be-will-be" philosophy, in time you will be one of them. Your dream will die, your vision will shrink, and your spiritual death will come.

Here is a test that will illustrate this. Suppose you tell your "average" friends that within five years you are going to be making $200,000 a year. Your "ordinary" friends will laugh. They will tell you that you're naive. Foolish. What's more, they will be eager to tell your other friends how silly you are for thinking you could make that kind of money. But tell people who are making $200,000 a year what you plan to do, and they'll say, "Great. That's wonderful. How can I help?"

Keep in mind also, some people who aren't making it don't want you to make it either. They want you to live a mediocre life because this makes them feel better about themselves. Misery loves company, so your "we're-going-nowhere" friends want you to surrender to mediocrity, too. Your negative associates want you to fail. If you succeed, make money, nd enjoy the "good" life, you make them feel uncomfortable. You become a traitor to their group. So, if you don't make it, they will feel better about themselves. But the prosperous people you know do want you to succeed. Prosperous and successful people know there is much to be shared.

As you grow your dreams, surround yourself with people who are positive. Positive people want you to win, to achieve, to enjoy the good life, to find genuine satisfaction, and to make a contribution to others.

Negative people, on the other hand, want you to accept life as it is, to be content with boredom and mediocrity, to be satisfied with a small income, and to miss out on the rewards that come from helping others.

Keep out the weeds and the bugs. Let's go back to your tomato plant. It will do poorly at best if weeds compete with it for the energy of the sun, water, and plant food. And given a chance, insects will eat away at it until it dies.

Your dream of financial freedom will attract weeds and bugs, too. Negative friends will sow weed seeds of "it won't work," "you're wasting your time." Some will make fun of you for having big goals. Others will tempt you with "live for today." Bugs will also appear to threaten your dream. A "friend" may want to borrow money or urge you to search for a "better" opportunity.

And a lot of weeds and bugs will come from the media. Expect to be bombarded with negative news about business, the economy, reports of business failures, congressional investigations, and changes in tax laws.

It takes great effort to separate oneself from negative people, but *you are almost certain to become wealthy if you affiliate with success-oriented people.*

So, decide right now to examine the people you associate with on a day-to-day basis. Divorce yourself from those who are bad-mouthing everything and want to see your dream die.

STEP V:
FOCUS YOUR ENERGY—PUT "I WILL" TO WORK

Vince Lombardi, one of football's great coaches, was famous for saying, "Nothing can stop the perfectly disciplined will." His winning record puts deep meaning into the maxim "Where there is a will, there is a way."

Coach Lombardi's outstanding contribution was to show what the power of will can do, not only to win football games, but to win life games as well.

Victories come from thinking "*I will* get what I want," not from thinking "I'd like to have something." You see, "*I will*" is the strongest commitment one can make. When you think *I will*, your mind performs two amazing acts: First, it shows you how to achieve your dreams and, second, thinking "I will" supplies the energy you need.

Look at it this way. All your mental power is in the "I will" part of your mind. The deeper you fix your dreams in your mind, the more certain you are to achieve your dream. Think "I *will* buy the home I want," and the source of financing will appear. Think "I *will* make my business idea a reality" and the how-to-do-it will come. Think "I *will* get a job promotion," and what you must do will become evident.

Once your "I will" is under your absolute control, winning games, making money, getting the mate you desire, winning the election — whatever you want — will be yours.

Everyone has an "I'll try" side and an "I will" side in his mind. When someone says, "I'll try," translated it means "I'll go through the motions but I'm sure I'll fail." The "I'll try" folks already are thinking subconsciously of an escape hatch or an acceptable excuse for giving up. The salesman who tells his manager, "Well, I'll try to see Mr. Brown, but I doubt that I can arrange it" isn't going to see Mr. Brown. But the salesman who says, "I will see Mr. Brown. I don't know how, but I will" is going to not only see Mr. Brown, but is going to sell Mr. Brown as well.

The point: To achieve any dream — wealth, admiration, business success, total dedication to the objective is required.

Focused energy determines who wins. Consider two tennis players in a championship match — both players have excellent records, both have about equal experience, both are in top physical shape, and both are the same age. Who is going to win? The person with the greater determination.

Columbus discovered the New World. Why? At that time, there were at least one hundred sea captains of equal skill, and many were talking about sailing west in the unchartered sea, but Columbus made the absolute commitment to seek a short cut to the Far East. For more than two decades, he focused his energy on his dream of sailing across the "ocean sea."

Charles Lindbergh was not the first pilot to think about flying solo non-stop across the Atlantic. But his "dream machine" was even better than his flying machine. His commitment made him first and won him the admiration of the world.

Van Braun was not the smartest nor best educated rocket engineer. But he was the most devoted, most inspired, and most committed. And he played center stage in our conquest of the moon. The American flag will be on the moon forever because his dream captured the imagination of other engineers and ultimately of the world.

WHO IS WINNING? T.P. OR J.E.?

Consider two men, Ted P. and John E., both in their mid-thirties. By any conventional measuring device, Ted's I.Q. is in the top one percent. Well educated, Ted has a Ph.D. He is handsome, healthy, happily married, and daddy to a fine daughter. Ted's interests range from physics to basketball to global politics.

Sounds like a description of an extraordinarily successful person? Wrong. An electronics engineer, Ted has had four jobs in six years. Ted is getting nowhere. The reason for each job dismissal is the same — "T.P. gets involved in too many projects, and he finishes nothing," "does not see a project through to completion," "wonderful guy, but does not move the ball."

The problem? Ted does not focus his energy. His mind is never all in one place.

Meanwhile, John E., on the surface, seems far less qualified than T.P. John has usual intelligence, doesn't have a degree, is overweight, and reads little (once in conversation, someone asked John, "Where are the Falklands?" John's reply, "Someplace in Indiana, I think").

Sounds like John is Mr. Strictly Ordinary. Right? Wrong!

John and his family are happy. John has his own business selling pleasure boats to dealers and earns a net profit of $250,000 or more every year.

What's John's secret? He loves boats — how they're built, what they can do, how to use them, and he believes that everyone should have at least one. Every room in John's house has some furniture, lamp, or painting that shows love for boats.

What's the key difference between Ted and John? Ted dissipates his energy while John concentrates his. Ted uses a pellet gun to shoot at many distant targets. John concentrates his energy into a rifle and shoots at one nearby target.

Do this. To make your dream happen, "zero in," "get your act together," focus your "I will" energy, and make a total commitment.

STEP VI:
HIRE TIME TO WORK FOR YOU

It is extraordinarily difficult for a small child to realize weeks or months must pass before a vegetable seed bears fruit. Or to understand that it may take decades for a small pine to become a giant tree.

It is, in fact, difficult for anyone at any age to see the wisdom and necessity of putting time to work for you.

INVEST TIME TO BUILD A CAREER

All dream seeds require time to produce the benefits you want.

Let me tell you about Rachel, a 20-year-old daughter of a friend of mine. She had a real dilemma. Rachel told me, "I would like to be a physician. My test scores will get me into one of the five top-rated medical schools."

"It doesn't sound like you have a problem at all," I replied. "Medical schools have very high standards; they reject about nine out of ten applicants."

"I know," Rachel agreed, "but going to medical school means ten years of enormous effort with no income. And the next ten years are the best of my lifetime. I'd like to travel, meet lots of people, do what most young people do. What should I do?"

"Well," I said, "work is a key part of your life. If you'd rather be a physician than anything else, be a physician. Ten years seem long but you'll enjoy the experience. And you'll still have about forty years left to practice."

A critical dream test all people face is, "Do I invest time and talent now for a higher reward later, or do I spend my time like most people and live only for today?"

INVEST TIME TO MAKE MONEY

You often hear the saying "It takes a lot of money to make a lot of money." Another old saying that isn't true is "The rich get richer and the poor get poorer."

In investing, time is actually more important than is the amount of money. One dollar isn't much, but invested at 12 percent with the earnings allowed to compound it will earn $32 in 30 years, $1,024 in 60 years, and $32,768 in 90 years.

The principle of plow back simply means you invest your return from an investment to earn more returns in the future. Look at this example to see how the enormous magic of plow back or compounding can, in time, produce a fortune.

Jane and Jill, age 25. Each make a one-time lump sum investment of $1,000 to return 18 percent per year in dividends and appreciation in value. At the end of every 12 months, Jane decides to take her return of $180 and buy something she "really" wants. Jill elects to add her $180 to her original investment of $1,000.

So, at the end of one year, Jane has $1,000 invested and the

$180 item she wanted so badly. Jill has $1,000 plus $180 working for her or $1,180 invested. If Jane continues to spend her profits each year and Jill continues to reinvest or plow back her profits, and the rate of return continues to be 18 percent, here is how their money picture will look down the road.

End of Year	Jane and Jill Are Age	Jane Has	Jill Has
4	29	$1,000	$ 2,000
8	33	1,000	4,000
12	37	1,000	8,000
16	41	1,000	16,000
20	45	1,000	32,000
24	49	1,000	64,000
28	53	1,000	128,000
32	57	1,000	256,000
36	61	1,000	512,000
40	65	1,000	1,024,000

At the end of 40 years when Jane and Jill are age 65, these are the results.

Jane will still have $1,000 plus 40 gifts each made to herself of $180 each or the equivalent of $7,200 (40 years x $180). Meanwhile, Jill has over one million dollars! Through the miracle of compounding, Jill's investment has increased 1,000 times. Even if Jill's money had been compounding at only 15 percent, she would have over $300,000 at age 65.

Compounding is the most important investment concept you need to know. Consider this: Only $100 invested every month at 12 percent is $308,097 in 30 years. In 50 years, $100 a month is over $3,000,000.

Remember, three things determine how much your money enrichment program will make for you — the amount you invest, the rate at which your money is invested, and how long you let your money work for you.

Know the "rule of 72." To learn how fast your money will double, simply divide 72 by the rate of return. If your money is invested at nine percent, it will double in eight years (72 divided by 9). If your money is returning you 18 percent, it will double in only four years (72 divided by 18).

Look at what a single investment of $10,000 at 12, 18, and 24 percent return compounded can make for you *if you let time work for you.*

Time at end of	12 Percent	18 Percent	24 Percent
12 years	$ 40,000	$ 80,000	$ 160,000
24 years	160,000	640,000	2,560,000
36 years	640,000	5,120,000	40,960,000
48 years	2,560,000	40,096,000	655,360,000

WHATEVER YOU WANT, A STEP AT A TIME WILL GET IT

Success, wealth, and happiness always are achieved in steps, never all at once. Consider these examples:

- The dream of a costly college education for a new child can be assured with only $50 per month invested wisely.
- An attractive body means many repeat visits to the health center and jogging trails. Fat can be lost only a pound at a time.
- A girl can become a national beauty queen by winning one beauty contest at a time with coaching and discipline in between.
- A football team can win the conference championship one good game after another good game after another good game.
- Pete Rose became the all-time leader in number of career baseball hits, one hit at a time. He concentrated on the immediate goal — make a hit. And the big dream — to set a new record — came true.
- Actors who concentrate on one scene at a time will become great actors.
- A fellow with only one leg literally ran across the country 3,062 miles to make his dream that handicaps are only in the mind come true. He did it by running only one step at a time.
- A manager got to the top of a company promotion

by promotion, not by a sudden leap upward.
- It took tens of thousands of rocket launches to learn all the lessons needed to go to the moon and return.

Remember the proverb "The longest journey begins with one step." A giant fortune begins with only a few dollars. A happy life is built one day at a time.

PUT THESE PRINCIPLES TO WORK, NOW!

- Firm up big, powerful images of what you can be, can achieve, and can own. Success is a dream acted upon.
- Think of life as a garden. We grow the seeds we plant.
- A seed always reproduces its own kind. Ask "What seed do I want to grow?" And "What is the profit potential of my dream?"
- Prepare your mind to accept your grand idea. Wash away the dust, grime, and grease; condition it to accept big thoughts.
- Plant a great dream. A fortune is only an idea acted upon. Never wait for conditions to be perfect.
- Nourish your dream seed with imagination, encouragement, and ideas. Let success-minded people help you.
- Focus your energy with I WILL! You will succeed, not just "try" to be a winner.
- Use time to advantage. Invest time to build a career. Use it to create wealth.

Chapter 2

Whistle While You Work!

Twenty years ago I attended a farewell luncheon for a college dean who was retiring. In his brief thank-you remarks, this fine gentleman revealed his insight for successful living. He said, "Friends, there are just two roads to happiness. One is love, the other is work. Now, to gain real satisfaction in life, do two things: First, practice love in every human relationship. Second, find work you enjoy and put 100 percent of your energy into doing it well. Love loving and enjoy working, and your happiness and prosperity will be guaranteed."

The old scholar was right. Love loving and enjoy working, and happiness, prosperity, and success are assured.

BREAK THE CHAINS OF CAREER SLAVERY

I talk with many people who are dissatisfied with their careers. When our conversation gets around to the question, "If you're so unhappy, why don't you find other employment?", I hear many excuses (they call them "reasons") for staying in their self-imposed job slavery. Here are the chains people use to bind themselves to work they don't like.

JOB CHAIN 1:
"I'M TOO OLD (OR TOO YOUNG) TO MAKE A CHANGE."

Lots of people stay in their job-prison 40 hours per week because they think they are too old to move out and do something they want to do. People who think this way should remember that Henry Ford, who became America's first billionaire, was basically a shade-tree mechanic until he was in his 40s. Ray Kroc was a moderately paid salesman until he was in his 50s and created the world famous McDonald's. Colonel Sanders was in his 60s when he started Kentucky Fried Chicken stores. And President Reagan was 70 when he was sworn in as President for his first term.

At the other age extreme, the founders of Apple Computers and Cabbage Patch Dolls were in their mid-20s when they started their enterprises.

What is the best age to begin a career or change careers? The age you are right now. Successful people disregard age in making work decisions.

JOB CHAIN 2:
"BUT MY PRESENT JOB PAYS REASONABLY WELL. I CAN'T AFFORD TO TAKE A CUT IN INCOME."

Last month, I had lunch at a fine Atlanta restaurant. My waiter greeted me by name and identified himself as a former student. "You probably don't remember me, but I took a class with you four years ago. Two years ago, I got my MBA in finance."

When I finished lunch, the waiter, obviously wanting to talk to me, said, "You probably wonder why I'm working as a waiter when I have an MBA, so let me explain. The best job offer I received was for $22,500. Here I make about $30,000 a year. I'm a good waiter and, at this restaurant, tips are very good. When the demand for people with an MBA in finance improves and salaries go up, I'll try to get a job where I can use my education."

"Well," I replied, "I am surprised to see you here. But let me assure you, it's not because you are, as some people would say, 'only' a waiter." (Then I explained that I, too, had been a waiter and also a truck driver, a hotel clerk, a farm worker, and a door-to-door salesman — and a good one.) I tried to make the point that all work *is* important and should be respected.

I told my friend if he really likes the restaurant business, by all means, stay in it. All work is honorable. But if he doesn't see his future in that industry, take a cut in income and take a job in finance.

I emphasized the point that in the long run people make the most money doing work that challenges them. Many people make the mistake of considering starting pay only and of ignoring potential income.

Two weeks later, I got a call from the former student. "I'm back in the market for a job in finance. That's what I really want to do."

The point: Think potential. Think long run. Think job satisfaction. Don't be tempted by immediate, short-run rewards.

JOB CHAIN 3:
"BUT MY FAMILY (HUSBAND, WIFE, OR PARENTS) EXPECTS ME TO DO SUCH AND SUCH."

You undoubtedly know women who want to follow a certain career but don't because their husbands object. And you probably know husbands who want to pursue other opportunities but don't because their wives say "No." And some children follow certain professions, not because they want to but because they feel pressured by their parents.

When either a wife or a husband denies the other in order to follow a preferred job or career, the person is acting selfishly, and the result of such denial often leads to deep conflict. Each person in the relationship should act generously to accommodate the other's interests and be willing to make sacrifices for mutual benefit. When both parties act generously toward the other and willingly make sacrifices, a successful result is assured.

In the ideal situation, wives and husbands join together in a common economic pursuit. Good husband-wife relationships were at their best when America was primarily an agricultural society. Why? Because the same economic goals were pursued and because interdependency kept the couple spiritually united.

Not many families today can enjoy the benefits of economic interdependency — the joy that comes from working together to achieve common goals. But many couples do find much happiness working together in their own retail stores, restaurants, day care centers, legal offices, medical clinics, and service enterprises.

Many parents want children to follow in their footsteps, especially those in the professions (medicine and law) and in family-owned businesses. But to encourage offspring to do what daddy or mother love to do is a mistake unless the daughter or son is attracted to the occupation. Let me cite an example.

About 15 years ago, I happened to have two students, both of whom were sons of funeral directors. A long-standing tradition in that profession is for a son to take over the enterprise. By coincidence, both sons took over their family's funeral enterprise. One of the young men relished the idea of being a funeral director; his business prospered. The other young man also took over his father's funeral home, but only because he felt strong family pressure to do so. Four years later, the business was failing and had to be sold for far less than its real value.

Forcing or using subtle pressure to cause a child to follow in a parent's pursuit is unwise for three reasons:

    1. No son or daughter can achieve success in a parent-directed occupation when he or she dislikes the activity.

    2. Children will resent the parental interference in their lives.

    3. Parents will be disappointed in the second-rate achievements that inevitably result. Wise parents understand that seeing sons and daughters succeed in a field of their choice is a source of great satisfaction.

JOB CHAIN 4:
"BUT THE FIELD I WANT IS OVERCROWDED."

Let me present a statement as forcefully as I can. Read it twice before you continue so it sinks into your subconscious. *No occupation is ever or will ever be overcrowded with highly qualified people who have a burning desire to succeed.*

Consider the practice of law. For a decade, fine people with the right aptitude and the right attitude for legal work have been told, "Avoid law, the field is overcrowded. Seven thousand lawyers quit the practice of law every year. We have twenty times as many lawyers as Japan. You'll starve if you try to practice law. Besides, the practice of law is no longer a profession. Read the ads lawyers put in newspapers."

It is true that *quantitatively,* the legal field seems crowded. But when you talk to judges, to partners in prestigious law firms and to legal scholars, you'll learn that *qualitatively,* there is no surplus of legal talent.

The problem is many people now practicing law are attorneys for the wrong reasons: (1) "I can make a lot of easy money," (2) "It's a good way to get into politics," and (3) "I can take advantage of some people who are ignorant of the law."

Now, there is plenty of business for people who become lawyers for the right reasons: (1) "I'm challenged by it," (2) "As society becomes more complex, there will be an increasing need for competent attorneys," and (3) "Law and what it stands for — justice — will always be a respected, honorable profession."

"The field is overcrowded" advice is now being given to people considering the ministry, college teaching, medicine, acting, and journalism as occupations. Well, no field will ever be overcrowded with people of superior attitudes toward the occupation and a deep desire to perform.

Keep in mind that career forecasters like all forecasters are often wrong. For example, when the government places more emphasis on national defense, forecasts for engineers rise sharply. But when defense expenditures are cut, people are told to avoid engineering.

Employment opportunities are dynamic, always changing. When World War II ended, no one foresaw the enormous demand for computers. The television, road building, jet aircraft, and lodging industries, now enormous sources of employment, were small industries. Today, few forecast the enormous future demand for people in genetics, travel, and new forms of recreation.

The point: To make a wise career selection, consider only the field you have a "burning desire" to enter.

JOB CHAIN 5:
"DON'T TAKE THAT JOB — IT'S DEAD-ENDED."

All across the nation, "help wanted" signs are in windows of fast-food outlets, drugstores, photography studios, supermarkets, and car washes — retail and service businesses of all kinds. And the newspaper classified employment pages offer jobs in every conceivable industry and occupation. Employment demand greatly exceeds employee supply.

At any given time, there are between seven- and ten-million people out of work. Why?

Overly liberal unemployment benefits are one reason. But the main problem is many people view the available jobs as dead-ended, or beneath them. (A recent community college graduate told me, "I didn't go to college to sell hamburgers at McDonald's.")

Many people are blind to opportunity and quickly conclude some jobs lead nowhere. The truth is there are no dead-ended jobs in a free society — just dead-ended people blind to opportunity.

Let me illustrate. The owner of the firm who picks up garbage at our house and 15,000 other homes started working as a helper when he was 18 years of age. Now 12 years later, he's a multimillionaire. Where others saw only a dirty, smelly, bottom-of-the-bottom job, he saw ways to improve services, increase productivity, lower costs, and, in the process, make money.

The point: All jobs have a future; all jobs are open-ended.

Look at your job as it can be, not as it is. Smart people look not at the job they have at present, but where it can lead. See what can be, not what is!

Many of the people who head some of our largest organizations worked their way up from the very bottom to the top of a company's management structure. I talked with one of them in Oregon recently. This person had no formal education beyond high school (but as president of a major electronics firm, he adopted a policy that pays the full costs of any employee who will go to college during the evenings).

"I came to the company when I was twenty," he explained. "I was put to work on an assembly line. To be honest, I hated the work. But I regarded it as an opportunity. If I performed well, I'd be promoted. I learned the job easily and then started making suggestions on improving the way we assembled components.

"It wasn't long before I was promoted," he continued. "And after mastering the next job, I began to ask questions and make suggestions that resulted in fast promotions. When I was thirty-eight, the board of directors named me president."

"You must be very proud," I commented.

"I am," my friend responded, "but I've still not succeeded in instilling a desire to move up into all of our people. As you know, the company pays for the costs of education for employees; we have very extensive fringe benefits; and we promote almost entirely from within. The people who do routine work are at least as happy as their counterparts in any firm on the West Coast.

"I'm dissatisfied," he went on, "because only a very few of our employees visualize themselves moving up. I've designed our organizational structure so there are no dead-end jobs. Yet, most people at the bottom think their jobs are dead-ended and make no effort to advance."

Remember, there are only dead-end people, not dead-end jobs.

All great businesses, from Delta Airlines to IBM to Bank of America, were small at one time. But they were guided by ordinary people with extraordinary goals and vision.

Those "unimportant" jobs like operating a check-out counter, registering guests at a hotel, waiting on tables, being a hospital orderly, driving a cab, and delivering packages are opportunities to learn. Increasingly, executives want people with hands on, up front, and grass roots experience for their managers of tomorrow. What really counts in the world of work is the knowledge gained from doing the work, not from reading about the work in textbooks.

WANT BETTER HEALTH? ENJOY YOUR WORK!

Everyone wants better health. This is great. We live in a wonderful world and our stay is brief at best. No one ever gets enough of life if they enjoy it.

But the most expensive question we face is "how." Each year we set new records for money spent on special diets, pills, jogging, health club dues, and vacations and on trying to look better, feel better, sleep better, and prolong life.

Somehow, in our search for healthier living, we've missed out on the number one element necessary for healthy, happy living — *work we enjoy*. There is a direct relationship between longevity and challenging work.

Work you enjoy is the best guarantee you can find for a long, happy, and healthy life.

The magazine *Nation's Business* did a survey asking its readers to select the ten top business people America produced in its first 200 years. One would guess a person would have to endure a lot of worry, enormously hard work, frustration, and other job-related difficulties to be one of our super-performers.

The survey respondents nominated people such as Edison, Bell, and Ford. Each of the top ten were responsible for the livelihood of tens of thousands of workers. Each was involved with raising and spending billions of dollars. And each was engaged in highly competitive industries, often cited in health magazines as a cause of early death.

What was the average age of death for these enormous achievers? Eighty-seven!

Winston Churchill, one of the great statesmen of this century, drank excessively, smoked a dozen cigars a day, and never jogged, lifted weights, or engaged in an exercise program. And Mr. Churchill ate what he wanted and as much as he wanted.

He directed Britain during its most difficult time, wrote books, spoke at every opportunity, and made countless difficult decisions. Churchill violated all the "rules" for good health except the one we overlook: *He enjoyed his work.*

Mr. Churchill died at age 91!

Few people work as hard as Bob Hope and George Burns. And they are going strong, well into their 80s. They don't need the money nor the applause. They have received thousands of honors.

What makes them go? What keeps them healthy? They love what they do.

LOVE YOUR WORK AND YOU BEAT STRESS

A few years ago, the nation's aircraft controllers went on strike. Their union made the usual demands — more money, better fringe benefits, and shorter hours. The main argument the union leader made to support their demands was the terrible "stress" the controllers had to endure. Directing traffic in and out of airports, the controllers complained, was so nerve shattering it drove many of them to alcohol, to other drugs, and to mental break-downs. Even the unusual "stress" of handling air traffic was responsible — so they said — for heart disease, high blood pressure, abused children, and broken marriages.

The cure the union proposed for all of these "stress-related" problems boiled down to "pay us more money." (How anyone was foolish enough to believe the controllers' stress could be cured with higher salaries is difficult to understand.)

When psychologists and psychiatrists examined a sample group of striking controllers who complained most strenuously of work-related stress, they discovered an important but simple fact: *The stress-prone controllers did not like their work.*They should never have been aircraft controllers in the first place.

The mind examiners also discovered something else. The controllers who didn't strike and didn't complain of stress enjoyed the challenge, responsibility, and excitement of their work.

One controller I know who worked at the Atlanta Airport — the world's busiest — told me he really liked his job. But, yielding to peer pressure, he went on strike. My friend made an interesting comment to me. He said, "You know, I experienced far more pressure walking that stupid picket line than I ever did helping launch or land three hundred to five hundred passengers a minute. I found it disturbing to carry a sign telling passengers how our lives were being ruined by stress, when I knew, in my case, it just wasn't true."

Because air traffic is essential to the nation, and because strikes by government workers are illegal, President Reagan told the controllers, "Go back to work or you're fired." Many of them elected to be terminated. The union's prediction of a rash of air crashes didn't come true. And as one who flies several hundred thousand miles a year, I was relieved to know that the controllers were replaced with people who enjoyed directing air traffic.

STRESS IS REAL TO THOSE WHO HAVE IT, BUT WHY?

Chances are you know people who complain of stress, and some of them define their problem more sharply as "burn out," a new psychiatric term that is growing in popularity.

Make no mistake, stress seems very real. People spend billions every year on pills, diets, exercise gimmicks, and medical visits to cure their problems. But drugs, jogging, lifting weights, and talking with medical people don't cure stress.

The real cure is so simple it goes undetected. Very simply — to cure stress, you must attack its cause. And *the cause of stress is performing work you do not find enjoyable, challenging, and beneficial to yourself and others.* People who complain of work-related stress are misfits. Briefly, they don't like their work. They feel incompetent, bored, out of place, inadequate, mistreated, threatened, or unappreciated.

A SURGEON GAVE THE SAME CURE FOR STRESS: LIKE YOUR WORK

Two years ago, I had major surgery on my left leg. The next day the surgeon visited me to make sure I was recovering according to plan. I thanked the surgeon for his successful effort. Then I asked how his nerves can tolerate doing five or six surgeries each week, handling post-operative chores, and dealing with relatives of his patients.

The doctor smiled and said, "I enjoy my work. I'm one of the nation's best for the kind of surgery I did for you. Now if I had to do what you do (speak to different groups almost every day), I'd be in a miserable state. I'd be scared to death making a speech.

"You see," the surgeon continued, "I take great pride in my work. I know I'm very good. Helping people live more enjoyable lives — and in some cases helping them live at all — is rewarding.

"In thirty minutes," the doctor went on, "I'm going to do a very unpleasant surgery. I have to remove a patient's right leg. I can't guarantee his survival but, after the surgery is over, I'll say a prayer thanking God for giving me the skill and stamina to help that fellow in his struggle to survive and recover."

"That sounds like very severe surgery, doctor. How will you feel if the patient doesn't make it?" I asked.

"Well," the doctor replied, "I'll still sleep soundly because I will have done my very best. I know the patient will be dead in three or four days unless I do the surgery. I believe God expects each of us to do our very best. That is what I will do. The rest is up to Him."

IF YOU LIKE YOUR WORK, THERE IS NO STRESS

After my conversation with the surgeon, I was moved to another room. Through my window, I could watch construction workers build a new wing to the hospital. Watching the work, I saw workers walking coolly and calmly on twelve-inch-wide steel girders 11 stories above the ground. A wrong step would mean certain death. For most of us, working under those conditions would produce real stress. But the workers liked what they did, so stress was not a problem.

Any job can be stressful if the person doing it does not enjoy the task. Someone not challenged by public education might go mad teaching school; a lot of us would break down if asked to kick a game-deciding field goal in an important football contest. And a student who takes a course only because it is required is much more likely to experience stress than the same student taking a course because he or she wants to.

I made a list recently of some kinds of work that would be extremely stressful for me. Maybe you'd profit from making your list. Here's mine:

- Driving a cab in New York.
- Working as a policeman.
- Preparing income tax returns.
- Being a divorce lawyer.
- Working as a draftsman.

The point: Doing the work you really enjoy is a key to happiness, success, and prosperity. Don't cripple your chances for the good life by doing work you don't like.

ARE MANAGERS NINE TIMES AS HEALTHY AS THEIR EMPLOYEES?

For many years in management seminars, I've asked attendees to write down two numbers: The number of days of work they missed last year because of sickness and the number of days the average employee under their supervision missed.

The answers were amazing. The typical manager was sick about two days, and the typical non-manager missed 18 days, nine times as many.

Why? The main explanation is managers are more satisfied with their work than non-managers. People who don't enjoy their work are likely to get "sick" at every opportunity so long as they do not exceed the number of sick days allowed by the union contract or company policy.

What's more, employees who do not like their work
- steal more company-owned property (such as merchandise and tools),
- cause most of the friction and conflicts,
- spread rumors that disrupt activities, and
- are the primary cause of low productivity.

WHAT'S THE REAL CAUSE OF ALCOHOLISM?

I have a friend who is part-owner and managing director of a leading alcohol rehabilitation center. The need for his services are enormous. At least ten percent of our population over age 20 is considered alcoholic. And the costs of alcoholism — accidents, absenteeism, mistakes at work, bad decisions, and broken homes — are at least double the cost of our national defense.

I asked my friend the real causes of alcohol addiction. He laughed quietly and said, "Well, alcoholism comes from drinking too much alcohol. But, seriously," he went on, "excessive drinking is only a symptom of a problem. It is not the problem.

"At our center," he explained, "we keep careful records, and we do in-depth psychological testing. We discovered that 70 percent of the people we treat are basically dissatisfied with their work. So, to ease the pain of work dissatisfaction, they drink more and more."

Then the director of the alcohol rehabilitation center made an observation that is especially meaningful to all of us. "Over the past fifteen years, we've treated one hundred and fifty-four ministers, rabbis, and priests for alcohol addiction. According to our analyses, seven out of ten did not enjoy being religious teachers. The great majority of them took up religious teaching because they felt pressured by their families to follow that calling.

"We've found work dissatisfaction is the bottom-line cause of most drug problems — not only alcohol. So, as part of our therapy, we place strong emphasis on vocational guidance to help our patients find work they enjoy."

"What about your cure rate?" I asked. "I understand a lot of people who take treatment sooner or later take up drinking again."

"You're right, but we have learned that those who follow our career guidance suggestions have a much higher cure rate than those people who don't like their work but return to it nevertheless."

ENJOY MAKING SACRIFICES: THEY ARE INVESTMENTS IN SUCCESS

A. P. Gouthey once wrote, "To get profit without risk, experience without danger, and reward without work is as impossible as it is to live without being born."

In that brilliant statement, we find one of the absolute essentials to living successfully.

Succinctly, there is no success without sacrifice.

But is sacrifice bad? Like many words in our language, the word "sacrifice" is misunderstood. To most people, sacrifice means giving up time or money, or enduring hardships, or doing something unpleasant. Now, it is true that sacrifice may mean those things. But that is only half the definition. The other part of the definition, the one that is almost always overlooked, is *to gain something even more valuable*.

So, the complete definition of sacrifice is give up something of value   money, time, or energy — to gain something of even more value — more money, a higher standard of living, better education for the kids, or other valuable considerations.

Or, very simply, sacrifice means give up a little now to receive more later.

Sacrificing then means investing. We give up something today so we will have more of something tomorrow.

Let me give you an example of how one executive I know, Jerome W., managed sacrificing for the benefit of his wife, four kids, and himself.

I have known Jerome since he joined a leading home products company as a salesman 25 years ago. His success with the company was phenomenal. About a month after he was named Chief Executive Officer, I had lunch with him. I asked Jerome to tell me if the sacrifices he and his wife and family made were worth the top job — the grand prize he had earned.

Jerome thought for a moment, and then he said something profound.

"Early in my career with the company," Jerome began, "I came to understand the wisdom in the old saying 'The chase is more fun than the kill.' I translated that to mean the trip to the top should be at least as much fun as being on top.

"You see," Jerome went on, "life is a trip and death is the ultimate destination for all of us. Now I think everyone will agree that living a life of adventure is more fun than dying in boredom for thirty or forty years. So, my wife Mary and I decided at the outset we would make my trip to the top of this company — and I'll make no bones about it, from the outset I did want to go all the way — a grand adventure."

"How many times did you move in the past twenty-five years?" I asked.

"Seven," Jerome replied. "That meant selling seven houses, buying seven houses, putting our four kids in seven different school systems, and adjusting to seven different communities."

"Most people would say that's too much sacrificing for anyone's career," I injected.

"What Mary and I did," Jerome explained, "was to make each move an adventure. We would help the kids look forward to each move as an opportunity to make even more friends, see more of the nation, look forward to different customs, climates, and ways people live. Sure, the kids would miss their friends for a while, but young people adjust quickly.

"And there were all sorts of prices I had to pay. I had to adjust to different managers along the way. Some were great people. A few were not. Sometimes I had people assigned to me who weren't made from the right stuff. And, on two occasions, I had associates who tried to stop my career advance by making me look bad. But I welcomed these experiences — they made me stronger."

What Jerome said to me boils down to this: Sacrificing is largely a state of mind. Most people consider being transferred to mean making a sacrifice. Jerome and Mary made it an adventure instead.

If sacrificing pays off, why do people go to extremes to avoid it? Why do people resist sacrificing? Why do people not want to forego today's pleasures for even more satisfaction in the future?

Perhaps it's the old attitude popular during war times when soldiers would say, "Eat, drink and be merry, for tomorrow you may die," or maybe it's the lingering holdover from the "now" generation which wanted its demands to be met immediately like an infant's instant gratification.

Anyone who wants to achieve maximum success must be willing to sacrifice or invest now for reward later.

To validate this point, consider the following:

- A majority of people reaching age 65 have little savings, investments, or other valuables — this after spending 45 adult years in the richest society ever known. Had these people in poverty and near-poverty invested only ten percent of what they had earned in one of hundreds of "sure" investments, they would be very well off financially, and the social security system could be phased out completely.
- Many young people feel that 35 or 40 hours a week is all they should work. Being asked to work more than that is such a "big" sacrifice, many try to find another job.
- Millions of people performing tasks that are rapidly being taken over by robots and computers think it's too much of a sacrifice to learn new skills that are increasingly in demand.
- Rather than invest part of what they earn, millions and millions of people give way to temptation and buy things on the no-money-down-48-months-to-pay plan.
- And millions of students, rather than sacrifice and really learn a subject, use every conceivable technique to pass a course except to learn the material.

Now, on the positive side, there are some people of all ages to be commended for their willingness — and good sense — to sacrifice.

Physicians are among the most respected people in society. Why? Because a person must make enormous sacrifices to qualify as a doctor. To become a physician, a person must earn superior grades in pre-med college and endure a grueling medical school program. Then comes the *real* sacrifice: Serve as a resident or intern in a hospital to get hands-on experience. For a low salary, the intern works 100 or more hours a week, goes without rest or sleep for

36 hours at a stretch, and gets only one day off per month. People who train physicians say this extraordinary work schedule is needed to teach new doctors to develop the discipline and sense of responsibility expected of physicians. Serving boot camp in medicine is tough, but those doctors who pass their internships take enormous pride in their achievement.

A young physician friend of mine, John Y., is an example. I've known him since he first started pre-med ten years ago.

Recently, he told me, "I've worked twelve to sixteen hours a day, seven days a week, since I started school. I don't mind the sacrifice — I remember you defined sacrifice as an investment. I'll soon be a practicing physician and make a large income by most people's standards. And then my old firends who have been nine-to-fivers for years will be jealous of me because I'm living better than they are."

John's observations made me think of other young people I know who are sacrificing now for a better return tomorrow. Pete W. works as a computer serviceman. His beeper is at his side 168 hours a week. He makes the service calls willingly because, "That's my job, I'm good at it, and my company believes in keeping customers satisfied."

And I know a woman, aged 32, who works full time as a secretary and part time as a waitress to help support a younger sister who suffers from an incurable kidney disease and requires very expensive treatments.

Sacrifice is an investment that means more than just money. Sacrifice means deep satisfaction in helping others to find joy in this world.

Remember the statement by A. J. Gouthey I quoted earlier? "To get profit without risk, experience without danger, and reward without work is as impossible as it is to live without being born."

Let me re-tell an old story. A very rich king wanted to summarize what it takes to become a success. He asked the wisest people in his kingdom to find the secret. "I'll give you ten years to come up with the answer," he said.

Ten years later, the wise people returned and put 24 books on the king's table.

"This looks too complicated," the king said. "Take ten more

years to find the real answer."

Ten years later, the brilliant scholars returned. This time they put only one book on the king's table.

"That's still too complicated," the king said. "I'll give you ten more years to find the answer to success."

Ten more years passed and the wise people, older and weary, returned and put one piece of paper on the king's table. On it was written, "There is no free lunch."

The king was elated, "Finally," he said, congratulating the wise people, "you have found the answer to success. There is no free lunch."

My friends, happiness, achievement, money, promotion, reward, love, and anything else of value are gained only through sacrifice.

Enjoy making sacrifices. They lead to success.

WANT MORE SUCCESS? PRACTICE MORE SACRIFICE

Many people believe professional athletes are overpaid, especially football players. But when sacrifices are considered, they may be underpaid! A tremendous amount of practice and sacrifice is required to earn a pro contract. Only one high school football player in 12,000 is ever considered. When the player gets a contract, even bigger sacrifices are required. One sacrifice — practice — is very demanding. A quarterback practices 100 pass attempts for every pass you see thrown on TV; plays may be practiced 50 times before used in a game. Other sacrifices involve being away from one's family, uncomfortable travel, injuries, and blows to the ego when performance is not up to expectations and the fans boo.

Sacrifices make athletes professional.

Outstanding performances by successful people look so easy. The speaker who wins a standing ovation, the artist whose paintings command high prices, the executive who makes it to the top, the salesperson who wins a national award — they all seem to achieve success with little apparent effort.

But go behind the scenes with successful people and you find enormous preparation. The piano player who thrills an audience may spend ten hours or more practicing for each hour performing. The great football players spend 20 minutes in practice for each minute they play.

Top performers make their work look effortless, and many people who listen to a concert may get the impression that playing the instruments is easy or that the performers simply have a natural instinct to make a beautiful sound. What observers don't realize is the amount of time and effort top performers put in everyday to develop their skills.

Anytime you see a doctor, musician, or speaker perform with no apparent effort, you are observing a person who has paid enormous sacrificial dues to become a superstar.

An old story illustrates why professionals earn more money: A company had a machine that wouldn't work. Employees tried everything they knew to fix it. Finally, the manager called in a consultant. The expert looked at the machine for a few minutes, took a rubber hammer from his kit, softly hit the machine in a certain spot, and, presto! the machine worked just fine.

Soon the manager got a bill for $300. The manager was perplexed. All the consultant did was tap the machine with a hammer. So he asked the consultant to itemize his bill. In short order, the consultant sent this bill:

Hitting machine with hammer .... $ 1.00
Knowing where to hit machine 299.00

Total $300.00

The point: Expert knowledge pays off!

How does one become a professional? Only from practice, practice, and more practice.

And when can a person be considered a professional? How much practice is required? Does a certain number of years in school qualify one to be a professional?

Here is the only meaningful criterion: *A person is a professional when he or she makes a task look so simple, so natural, so easy that anyone could do it.*

A nurse who can extract blood from a hard-to-find vein of a patient and cause no pain is a professional. So is the diver who jumps 60 feet and causes no splash. And the teacher who explains gravity to eight-year-olds so they understand it is a pro.

Every occupation needs professionals — people who do their tasks with finesse, expertise, and dedication. And in every field, from work in a fast-food restaurant to performing dental surgery to computer programming, it is the professionals who get the most rewards.

DOES EXPERIENCE MEAN A PERSON IS COMPETENT?

A placement specialist told me about a problem people in her profession have in matching people with jobs. "Today," she explained, "most résumés are prepared by experts for a fee. It's getting harder and harder to determine a person's real qualifications because of the way most résumés look and read. A key point those of us in placement recognize more and more is that 'experience' and 'ability' often do not equate."

I asked her to explain.

"Well," she went on, "experience can be very misleading. For example, five years' experience may only mean a person has been employed five years but has learned nothing for the past four years. Experience measured only by years-on-the-job in no way indicates a person's expertise.

"It often happens," my friend continued, "a person with two years' experience has grown more and is more valuable than a person with ten years' experience. What really counts in moving up today is how much a person *gains* from time spent on a job — not just the amount of time put in."

The point: To command the best monetary and psychological rewards, and to resolve to go through practice and commitment. Time spent on a job without growth ends up as time wasted.

ENTREPRENEURS SACRIFICE, TOO

Most millionaires are self-made. Most millionaires did *not* inherit their wealth. Of the 1 million millionaires in America, 81 percent made their fortunes in their own businesses.

And succeeding in your own business demands sacrifice. When the typical person sees a self-made millionaire, he or she jealously assumes luck made the person rich. They are right *if* we assume luck means doing without for a time in order to have a nice home, fancy cars, and expensive vacations, and to work 70 to 100 hours a week, risk one's savings in the business, borrow more money, and forego "pleasures," such as TV, reading, and time with friends.

HOW TO SELECT THE RIGHT CAREER

You will spend more time in your life working than doing anything else. And the quality of your work life directly affects the quality of your life with your mate, children, and friends. You like yourself in proportion to how much you like your work, and how much success, wealth, happiness, and health depend on your work.

Two key questions for finding the right career are:

1. Will rewards be based on performance?
2. Does the job expand as your ability expands?

ARE REWARDS BASED ON PERFORMANCE?

A key question in selecting a job is "Will my rewards — pay, bonuses, fringe benefits, promotions — be based on my performance?" In other words, if you do a great job, will you be paid more than if you do only a good job?

Common sense tells us all pay plans should be based on how well the job-holder performs the work. But this often is not the case. Let me share an example which, chances are, you've seen, too.

Jill, Bob, and Fran work as cashiers at a supermarket. Their jobs are the same: Greet the customer positively, add the cost of the items, accept payment, bag the items, and say, "thank you" cheerfully. Jill glows with enthusiasm and energy and serves 150 customers during a shift. Bob is average all the way, puts out only a mediocre effort, and serves 100 customers. Fran exhibits an "I'm-only-here-because-I-have-to-eat" effort and serves 50 customers. Now, it's payday and guess what? All three paychecks are for the same amount.

It may seem unfair, but a lot of people are not rewarded for what they produce. In this example, Jill subsidized Bob and Fran.

One situation where rewards do equate with performance is commission sales. Commission salespeople are paid on the basis of how much they sell. (What could be a more logical system? The objective of selling is to sell.) Entrepreneurs are also rewarded on how good a job they do in generating income for their business and controlling its costs. Doesn't it make sense to find out before you go to work for anyone whether your extra effort will be rewarded?

Two areas in which there is little, if any, correlation between rewards and performance are employment in government and education. You likely know some dedicated government employees who put forth their best professional effort but are not paid as much as their associates who do virtually nothing. The same is true for teachers. In both the government and education bureaucracies, more rewards are often given for years of service than for the quality of work performed.

Unless other factors outweigh the monetary rewards, intelligent people opt for careers in other fields.

DOES THE JOB EXPAND YOUR ABILITY?

Before you take a job, ask yourself, "Will I be a more valuable person six months, a year, three years from now?" If you're thinking of giving up your present job, ask, "Have I learned something useful in the job I have?"

If the answer to the first question is "No," don't take the position. If the answer to the second question is "No," relocate as soon as you can.

Serve your apprenticeship with the best. Everyone needs a "learning center" — a place to acquire the knowledge, skills, and techniques to prepare for what he or she wants to do. Smart football players who want to join the pro ranks choose colleges from which most players are recruited. Aspiring physicians select the most respected medical school, and people who want to learn the ins-and-outs of the computer field serve an apprenticeship with a top-rated computer company.

The basic consideration in choosing a job is not the starting pay, but, rather, what you can learn that will help you move up or prepare you to start your own enterprise.

Most law and accounting partnerships, advertising agencies, medical practices, and consulting firms are started by people who learned the necessary skills working for another firm.

The key question in evaluating any job opportunity is, "What can I learn that will prepare me for either my own business or an upscale promotion in this field?"

Many people hurry through college only to serve an apprenticeship where they learn little or nothing they can use to move up. No learn means no good.

Find a coach or mentor who can teach you the most. Great actors sharpen their skills working under great directors; few, if any, outstanding football players get to the top without a great coach. Outstanding salespeople are taught the basic techniques by outstanding sales managers.

Keep this in mind: If you already know more than the person you report to, you're wasting your time.

And be willing to go to "boot camp." The military services use boot camp to indoctrinate new personnel. The training and discipline are rigorous. The main purposes of boot camp are to provide basic training and to evaluate the individual for a future assignment. But another key objective is to determine if the recruit can "take it." Some individuals cannot, and they are released.

But there are also boot camps for civilians. I'm thinking now of the Southwestern Company, an organization based in Nashville that recruits thousands of young college people to sell biblical literature during the summer. After a few days of intensive training in Nashville, they are sent all across the country to sell the products. And it is tough. They start early in the morning and they work until late at night selling direct to the consumer.

The young salespeople work on straight commission. And they hear "no" much more often than "yes" when they ask for an order. But they learn the basics of effective selling much as the marine in boot camp learns how to survive in combat.

I've met many of Southwestern's alumni over the years and almost always they turn out to be highly successful people in business and the professions. Their summers as Southwestern representatives are high points in their lives. They learn how to survive and succeed. The products are great and the leadership is excellent, but *success still boils down to the individual.* The individual has to make it on his or her own.

In quick review:

- Break the chains of career slavery.
    - a) You are the right age if you want to make a job change.
    - b) Future pay is more important than present pay.
    - c) People closest to you want you to be pleased with your job.
    - d) Every field is wide open for people who give their best.

- Want better health? Enjoy your work.
- Love your work and beat stress and other ailments.
- Sacrifices are investments in success; making them is rewarding.
- In choosing a job, make sure pay and rewards are based on performance.
- Choose a job that helps you to grow and to maximize your talents.

Chapter 3

The Magic of Thinking Big

When I was going to college, I decided to attend a different church each weekend for one year. I was determined to expose myself to as many different faiths, beliefs, and concepts as I could, hoping I'd find what we all seek — a practical, workable success philosophy. One Sunday, I was on my way to a certain church when I passed another place of worship. The bulletin board on the lawn promised a sermon so intriguing I decided to visit it instead.

The sermon title was a real grabber: "The Biggest Temptation of All." I was young and already had some ideas about temptation. Early in his sermon, the minister explained what the biggest temptation was *not* — not lust, not greed, not stealing, and not lying. He told the congregation that the biggest temptation was to accept the petty value system of small-minded, jealous, and negative people. The minister emphasized that if we conquered this temptation, handling other temptations would be relatively easy.

Over and over, he stressed this point: *Put your life in proper focus.* Concentrate on what is really big in relating to others, your family, your career, your money, and your goals.

I remember that sermon today, decades later, as if I had heard it this morning. Let me share my understanding of that great message with you. The wisdom that minister gave us will help you in your quest for success, wealth, and happiness.

PUT SOME FROSTING ON THE CAKE
GIVE PEOPLE MORE THAN THEY EXPECT

What is special about a good cake? The frosting, of course — the extra-sweet icing that is put on the cake after it's baked. Some bakeshops do a thriving business baking cakes and then decorating them to your liking. A few months ago, my granddaughter Sara was quite ill. I bought her a cake and had the lady in the bakeshop write on it "Glad You're Getting Well, Sara." (Notice that I wanted Sara to see herself not as being sick but as getting well.) The cake (but more importantly, the message on the frosting) was worth a ton of medicine. And seeing Sara's eyes and hearing her gleeful voice when she saw her personally decorated cake put some new vigor in grandpa, too.

There's a money-making success-producing lesson in putting frosting on the cake. Two years ago, we had a hard freeze. The pipes froze. No water. So I started calling plumbers. The first five gave me the negative answer, "We've got more calls than we can handle. We can't possibly get to you for forty-eight hours or longer." Finally, plumber number six said, "Look, I've been going for forty hours straight. But I know about where you live and I want to help you. If you'll leave your lights on and tell me where the key is, I'll be there between one and two in the morning."

I was still working when the plumber came shortly after 2:00 a.m. In short order, the water system was working and the plumber left. But the incident didn't end there. Four days later when the cold weather had gone, I got a call from the plumber, "Just wanted to check to see if the pipes are OK and that there are no leaks."

I told him that everything was working just fine. Then he said, "I sure was glad to be of service. Mr. Schwartz, I'm also in the air-conditioning business. If you need service this summer, just call and I'll be right there."

As fate would have it, in June the air-conditioning system broke down, and the plumber who had made the time to fix the frozen pipes naturally got the job. Why? Because he followed up his service call during the cold snap with a "Is-everything-OK?" phone call.

The plumber put frosting on the "cake" and got more business.

HOW A YOUNG DENTIST USES A LITTLE FROSTING TO BUILD HIS PRACTICE

Not long ago, my dentist of 25 years told me that he was retiring and had sold his practice to a young dentist who had only recently graduated from dental school. My long-time dentist assured me his replacement was very competent and suggested I see him for future needs.

Soon, I had a dental problem and made an appointment with the new dentist. Frankly, I was very apprehensive. But I found the young dentist to be professional and confident.

The next day, a Saturday, I got a phone call. "This is Bill Wilson, your dentist. I'm just checking to see if you're OK." Then he made a couple suggestions and told me how pleased he was to be of service.

Imagine! A dentist calling to make sure everything is OK. That call was the frosting on the cake. It proved the dentist was interested in my post-recovery.

That three-minute phone call ensured the new dentist of my continuing patronage for years to come. And the next time I'm asked "Can you recommend a good dentist?", one name will immediately come to mind. Over the years, that one phone call will produce thousands of dollars of income for the dentist.

How does one develop a successful dental practice? Put some frosting on the cake. Simply give more service than is expected.

HOW A LITTLE "FROSTING ON THE CAKE" IS BUILDING A REAL ESTATE BUSINESS

Put service first and money takes care of itself. That is a law of success just as certainly as gravity is a law of physics.

A friend who sells residential real estate follows up every sale with a goodwill, frosting-on-the-cake call on the buyer. "This is unusual in the real estate business," she explained. "Most agents are afraid the buyer will have some complaining to do. Often people do have minor problems. And I solve them. Nothing is better for my reputation than post-sale service. In a way, I'm glad when people have a complaint. People soon forget the agent who just sold them their house. But they remember the agent who gave after-sale service.

"And you'd be surprised," she continued, "how many times people I sold a house to contact me in a few years explaining they are being transferred or want to move to a larger home and ask me to sell the house I sold them. I've sold one house three times since I got into this business thirteen years ago."

Post-sale service — that little extra frosting on the transaction — pays. Just give a little more than people expect to get.

WHY JOHN SELLS TWICE AS MUCH APPAREL

The wholesale apparel business is as competitive as any I know. Some days a small apparel retailer has more salespeople in the store trying to sell him or her more merchandise than there are customers. Few apparel salespeople make it big, but John S. does.

One day, I asked John why he was making over twice as much money as the typical apparel wholesale salesperson made.

John thought for a moment and said, "Education."

Then I said to John, "That surprises me. I know education is a key factor in some people's achievements, but rarely do they mention it up front."

John laughed and said, "I didn't make myself clear. I didn't mean my education is responsible for me being a big earner. I went to night school for only a few quarters. When I said education, I was referring to what I do to help my retail customers re-sell the merchandise I sell them.

"You see," John explained, "my sale really isn't complete when the merchant takes delivery of the merchandise. That's only half the sale. The other half takes place when the merchant's customers buy what I sold the merchant. Many of my accounts are not good merchandisers. They don't know how to sell. And if they don't sell what I sell them, my business would dry up fast. So, when I present a new line to my customers, I tell the retailer what type of woman is a prime prospect for the garment — her age, her fashion-consciousness, her income, — those sorts of things. Then I explain what features of the garment to stress, how to demonstrate the item and, most important of all, how to capture the consumer's imagination."

"What do you mean, capture the consumer's imagination?" I asked.

John laughed and replied, "Most people who sell women's and

men's apparel sell only cloth. 'This is made of 100 percent wool' or 'This garment won't shrink if you wash it.' Now, statements like those don't sell. The merchant is only repeating what's on the label. What I teach my retail accounts to do is to tell the consumer how good this garment will make them look at work or how expensive people think it is when it really isn't, or to say, 'You look so trim in that dress.' That's what I mean by imagination. When I've put imagination into the retailer's mind, they sell more and I sell more.

"It's basically very simple. But most of my competitors just assume, and falsely, the retailer will automatically figure out ways to move the merchandise. So, answering your question, that's why I make about two times as much as the average guy on the road does."

Attention salespeople: Put some frosting on the cake for your customers. Help them resell the products and they'll do more business with you.

WANT MORE? WHATEVER YOU DO, GIVE SOMETHING EXTRA

An obstetrician told me why he calls each of his recently delivered mothers shortly after they leave the hospital.

"It's strictly a goodwill call because care of the mother and the infant now is in the hands of other specialists. But I make the call, anyway, for selfish reasons. I want the new mother to tell her friends about me when they become pregnant."

After settling a claim, business-building insurance agents call or visit the policyholder to make sure he or she is satisfied. And, since the policyholder is now aware that the insurance company does pay, the call is a perfect time to review the policyholder's other insurance needs. Settling a claim is a terrific opportunity to sell more insurance.

Smart people in all fields add some frosting to the cake they sell. Computer companies who want to earn a large market share follow up after the sale to make sure the installation is OK. I know a clothing salesman who calls his customers about a month after they have bought a new suit to ask them if it is satisfactory and, during the call, tell them about some new apparel the store just received.

Betty M. sells a variety of products for the home — detergents, silver polish, carpet cleaner, deodorants. She makes a call once a month to each of her customers to ask how the products are working and to suggest other products the homemaker may need. "Sure," she says, "our products are the best available. And some customers call me to place their orders. But to make my business grow, *I call them*"

Students who want better grades prepare their reports with a few extras as good typing and neat folders, and they spell the instructor's name correctly.

Putting frosting on the cake means giving people more than they expect to receive, and it begins with simple things like answering the telephone. More often than not, when you dial a business phone you hear someone say, in effect, "I don't like my job. Why did you bother me? Now what do you want?" The person's voice tone reveals perfectly the attitude of the person answering as well as the attitude of the business.

A smart business manager never places negative people in up-front jobs, such as telephone operator, receptionist, check-out stand cashier, and ticket seller. The customers and clients a business serves rarely, if ever, see the firm president or a key manager. They judge the business rightly or wrongly by the way they are treated by the "unimportant" people.

Experienced travelers stay at hotels where the reservationists are polite and positive; people choose restaurants based on the attitudes of people who seat them, serve them, and take their money. How good the food tastes is always less important than the service in building repeat patronage. And the companies that deliver packages know courteous, friendly service is their best competitive weapon in beating the Postal Service where, generally, counter personnel are negative in attitude.

Words and phrases as "please," "thank you," and "you look *good* today" are free frosting that make sales and build businesses.

Note to managers: Call your business or office. If you don't hear a wonderful "I'm-really-glad-you-called" voice, train or replace the person. Have a friend stop in at your business. If he doesn't get great service, take corrective action.

Success-oriented people ask, "How can I give others more than they expect? What kind of frosting can I put on the cake I'm selling?"

A cake—the product or service you offer—is just baked dough. But when you put some frosting on it and give it a little post-sale service, you've made the dough delicious. Try it, and enjoy the rewards.

TO INFLUENCE PEOPLE
USE THE "OPTIMUM-RESULT" APPROACH

A few months ago, I had breakfast in Minneapolis with a young friend, Alec W., who operates his own meeting-planning service. He plans major corporate meetings and arranges for the facilities, the entertainment, the speakers, the prizes, and the transportation for the attendees — all the details that are part of a successful meeting. At breakfast, Alec said to me, "It's three hours till your flight. I have to make a call on a prospective client. Would you join me? Maybe you could give me a pointer or two about making a sales presentation."

I said I'd love to if I would not be in the way.

Alec handled himself beautifully. He began by asking the prospective client to describe the optimum result he wants from the meeting. Alec said, "Mr. Brown, assume the meeting is over and the attendees are returning home. How do you want them to perceive the company, your goals for next year, the new product line? Ideally, what do you want the meeting to accomplish?"

Alec built his entire presentation on getting the prospect to describe the "optimum result."

When Alec finished probing for the optimum result, he carefully restated the major goals the prospect had for the meeting. Then he thanked the prospect and set a time he could return to present a comprehensive plan for the corporate meeting.

Later Alec explained, "With new prospects, I always use a two-interview approach. During the first interview, I simply gather information. I never try to tell a prospect how good my services are before I diagnose what the prospect wants and needs. On the second interview, I show how my services will help the prospect achieve his objectives."

On my flight home, I couldn't get Alec and his ultra-effective sales method out of my mind. Alec did not tell the client, "Here is what is best for you" or "We've got just the program for your meeting." Instead, Alec was a diagnostician. He let the prospect describe what the prospect wanted the meeting to accomplish, then Alec designed an ideal program to satisfy his prospective client.

Use the optimum-result approach to get a job. A lot of emphasis is placed on rēsumēs to get a job. Now, in truth, a rēsumē only helps you get an interview. It doesn't get you the job. The personal interview does that. And in the interview, you can use Alec's "optimum-result" method to advantage.

Here is how.

Early in the interview say something to the interviewer such as, "I know we're meeting today because you want to look me over to see if I am right for you, and I want to see whether your company is right for me. We're meeting to see whether an employment relationship would be mutually beneficial. Sir, would you describe the ideal person (optimum result) you have in mind?"

That is a frank but fair statement, and your prospective employer will say something similar to, "The person we want must have several qualities: honesty, competency, initiative, willingness to cooperate, and ambition."

Now, when you know what qualities the prospective employer wants, you can explain how well you measure up against his or her ideal standards. Give evidence of your honesty by mentioning you have been trusted with money or merchandise. Show that you are competent because of related work experience, education, and honors you've received.

When you ask the employer to describe the optimum or best person for the job, you show mature intelligence and you then can demonstrate your assets as they relate to the employer's needs. You have also proved to the employer you are businesslike in applying for the job.

HOW THE OPTIMUM-RESULT APPROACH
SOLD $1,500,000 WORTH OF REAL ESTATE

After hearing Alec use the optimum-result method successfully,

I began to incorporate it in selling clinics, always mentioning from whom I learned it. About 18 months after I explained "optimum-result selling" to a group of real estate agents, I met Jack A., a Los Angeles real estate agent.

Jack told me how he had put the method to work. "I got a call shortly after your seminar from an executive in Pittsburgh who was moving to Los Angeles to set up a branch office for his company," Jack began. "I decided to use the optimum-result sales approach. Instead of talking to him for five or ten minutes and then promising I'd send descriptions on several of our homes, I asked him to give specific details of what he wanted. After a one-hour diagnostic call, I knew how secluded he wanted the home to be, the kind of neighbors he wanted, and how close he wanted to be to shopping centers, schools, and golf courses. I learned everything my prospect felt was important. I promised him I'd look at our inventory of two thousand one hundred-sixty homes and get back to him in two days.

"Two days later I phoned and told the prospect that I had found four houses that met his requirements and urged him and his wife to visit Los Angeles the next weekend.

"I met the prospect and his wife at the airport Saturday morning, took them to lunch in the part of town where the four houses were located. Then I showed the four houses. In three hours the couple had made their choice and the sale was made."

"But you said you sold one million five hundred dollars using the optimum-result technique. Did this fellow pay that much for a house?"

"Oh, no," the agent smiled, "but over the next six months five other families were transferred here. And, since I had served the head person so well, it was only natural that he recommended me to his staff, so I ended up selling six houses."

I also explained the optimum-result approach to a friend who is building his own multi-level marketing business. People in his organization begin part time selling products, and invite other people to join his business.

To recruit people, he asks them to describe the ideal part-time business they would like to own. My friend tells me that what people want in their own part-time business are unlimited earnings, family involvement, flexible hours, low overhead, and products that are of real value.

"After I've gotten people to commit to what they want," my friend explained, "it's simple to show how my business fits their interests perfectly."

The optimum-result method works! Use it.

A major software company uses the optimum result to get more business from its 2,000 customers in the U.S.A. and Europe. Twice a year, the company invites its customers to attend a "convention" at *their own expense*! The purpose of the meeting is to give the customers an opportunity to tell the software producer what changes they want to see in existing products and what new products they feel are needed. In this way, the software company cuts way back on its marketing costs and builds enormous customer loyalty.

PRACTICE ASKING, "WHAT'S YOUR OPINION?"

A key part of the optimum-result method is to get people to express themselves. Everyone has an opinion about a lot of things: What the company is doing, right or wrong; what's good and what's bad about the economy; how the governor, the mayor and the president are performing; and whether social security will survive.

And many people in a business have opinions about how the enterprise could be better run. The problem is, in most organizations the people who do the work are never asked, "What is your opinion?" "Got any ideas for doing this better?" and "Can you suggest a way to do this in less time?" As a result, a large amount of intelligence is untapped, the people with ideas feel frustrated, and the organization's performance suffers.

I have a friend in Florida, Peter F., who is in the steel fabrication business. During the last recession, most steel companies had desperate problems. But Peter's business boomed. I met Peter a month ago at his company's resort hotel. I asked him why his business never stops growing while his competitors are in trouble.

"I guess a number of things explain it, but one thing I do is get the opinions of my people before making key decisions. Sure, I read *The Wall Street Journal* and other business publications regularly, but, as I learned in the Army, the best intelligence often comes from front-line soldiers. We install the steel we fabricate all over the country. I make it a point to talk with the installation crews. I ask for their opinions about what our customers are thinking. I maintain a steady flow of opinions, gathering information from our installation and sales people.

"We supply a lot of custom-designed refrigerated steel warehouses to customers. I'm always asking our present customers what changes they'd like to see in the next generation of refrigerated storage facilities.

"All people think," my friend went on, "so I encourage them to tell me what they're thinking about. When I ask for opinions from installers, truck drivers, production employees, or customers, I accomplish two things. First, I win their cooperation because they've had a chance to give me their views. Second, I pick up a lot of good ideas I can turn into profit.

"I've had some problem teaching the what-is-your opinion techniques to a few of my managers. Some of them are conditioned to believe that asking other people, particularly subordinates, for their ideas is a sign of weakness. To me, letting other people express their opinions is a sign of strength."

Use the optimum result. It works wonders in getting what you want — a sale, a better job, and cooperation and support.

- Find out what is the ideal benefit the other person seeks.
- Tailor what you have to offer to provide that ideal benefit.

You can use the optimum result in everything you do.

If you're a student and want to earn an A, ask the instructor at the beginning of the course specifically what is required to make an A.

If you're a lawyer helping someone make a will, learn exactly what the client wants the will to accomplish before you draft it.

If you want a promotion six months from now, ask your manager to tell you what will be required of you to earn it.

THINK QUALITY (IT PAYS), NOT QUANTITY (IT COSTS)

There is a subtle but significant difference between average people (be satisfied with little) and the folks who are dedicated to enjoying more. Success-oriented people put quality first in everything they do, from making purchases to developing friendships. Meanwhile, average individuals concentrate their attention on quantity. Success-directed people seek real value; average-directed people consider only "How much does it cost?" "How big is it?" and "What was the 'original' price?"

Avoid Bargainitis. I've conducted a little experiment over the years that may seem silly but, nevertheless, makes a point. In a classroom or conference, I've asked the women attending to write on a piece of paper the approximate number of pairs of shoes they own.

The average number is 24! Then I ask another question. "How many of your shoes have you worn in the past six months?" The average is usually four or five.

Finally, I ask, "Why did you buy so many shoes and not wear them?" The answers are about the same. "They were on sale and I just couldn't resist," or "The shoes looked great in the store but I soon discovered I didn't like them," or "They were marked down fifty percent."

In doing this experiment, I've also learned that the shoes that were bought but hardly ever worn were poorly made, were of low quality, and were of a current fad design. The shoes women wear most are of high quality (relatively expensive) and are well fitting and attractive.

I've done similar experiments with men about their shirts and ties. The conclusions are the same. Most men wear only a fraction of the shirts and ties they own. And the I-bought-it-because-it-was-on-sale motivation also stands out.

Perceptive shoppers own comparatively few of anything. They know that *real* bargains are not "on sale" or "good buys." Smart buyers know the wisdom in the observation "pay twice as much and buy half as many."

The quality dress purchased today will still be in style a decade or two from now. A quality car will still be valuable and will still be admired five or ten years from now, when today's "special deal" will be worthless. Quality jewelry gains in value as time passes; bargain jewelry bought today has no value tomorrow.

Translated, "It's on special sale" usually means "It's not very good."

Some estimate that 30 percent of all the food purchased "because it is on sale" goes into the disposal or garbage can. One of the simple tricks some detergent makers use is to package their products in extra large boxes, then fill them mainly with inert substances to suggest a "big bargain." Regardless of what you buy — clothing, appliances, automobiles, food, even a house — be extra careful about purchasing simply because it's on sale. The concept "Don't be penny-wise and pound-foolish" advocated by Benjamin Franklin still holds true.

A whole new industry — mini-warehouses — has grown up largely to help people store products they wish they hadn't bought but would feel guilty if they threw away. Small apartments and condos aren't the problem — inability to resist temptation to buy what amounts to junk is.

More friends or real friends? A few summers ago I met a former congressman at a resort in Colorado. We both had addressed a human resources conference. Later, we spent a couple hours talking about life's greatest mystery — people.

"I was in Congress for twelve years," my new acquaintance told me. "During that time I thought I had thousands of friends. Every week, I got hundreds of letters and dozens of phone calls. When I visited my district I was besieged by well-wishers. I had no trouble raising money to campaign.

"Then," the former congressman said, "I learned a big lesson only hours after I was defeated in my seventh campaign. (At this point, the former legislator held up both hands, palms toward me and fingers spread apart.) I discovered I didn't have ten real friends in the whole world."

"There must be a lesson in your experience," I commented.

"There is," my friend explained. "After I had time to think about it, I concluded it is better to have ten real friends than ten thousand people who are for you when you're on top but ignore, even scorn, you when you're down. Friends, like everything else, should be measured by their quality, not by their quantity."

The aging gentleman made an important point: When it comes to friends, count only those who truly care about you and want to help you, expecting nothing in return. Never count among your friends people who only want a favor from you.

Less price is worse value in real estate. Real estate is about the most nearly perfect investment or business one can find. Real estate is the only kind of property that is truly permanent. That's why it's called "real." No more of it is being made. It is the source of everything we eat, wear, use, and live and work in. Yet, when it comes to buying or renting real estate to live in, many people put price ahead of value, and they end up short-changed.

Selecting a residence can be a prolonged, difficult, even tortuous experience. And when the purchase decision is finally made, many buyers are soon displeased. Often discussions like this take place between a couple who has purchased a house.

She: "It's not my dream house, but I guess it's adequate for our needs. Besides, our combined income is not that great and our jobs aren't guaranteed. We could have bought the house we wanted, but the agent stressed that this place is a bargain."

He: "I agree. Frankly, the place doesn't look like much and I'm kind of embarrassed. But with some luck, our income will increase, and maybe in four or five years we can move to a place we like better."

She: "I hope so. Jimmy's only four now, so I guess the neighborhood will be good enough for him until then."

He: "Maybe we could have bought a nicer house but we'll try to be satisfied with this one. After all, times are very uncertain."

Is the compromise these people made worth the cost? The couple doesn't really like the house, so they will give it less care and make fewer improvements. The child already is at an age when the physical environment and the influence of other children is enormously important. Because the house is not located in a highly desirable area, appreciation will be less than a home in a nice area. In fact, the house may even depreciate.

Where we live influences every aspect of life — our attitudes, our confidence, our friendships, even our health. People who decide to go first class in choosing real estate are happier, grow more prosperous over time, and feel better than folks who go the skimp-and-compromise route.

Avoid the paper clip mentality. There are only two basic questions people must answer correctly to accumulate great wealth.

The first is:

"How can we increase revenue or income?"

The second wealth accumulation question is:

"How can we reduce expenditures or cut costs?"

Every decision made in managing personal or business finances involves answering these two questions.

When it comes to keeping expenditures in line, many people adopt a "paper clip mentality." On dozens of occasions, I have observed business executives discuss ways to trim costs or keep expenditures in line. And almost without exception, the conversation soon centers on cutting back on relatively unimportant matters, such as office supplies (legal pads, envelopes, paper clips) and travel, and raising the thermostat in summer so everyone is too warm (and less efficient) and lowering it in winter so people are too cold (and less efficient).

Meanwhile, these cut-back-on-little-expenditures efforts often overlook the big ways to deal with expenses such as eliminating unprofitable products, combining some departments, making better use of computers, and selecting new vendors.

It has been said, "Americans know the price of everything but the value of nothing." We see this truism in action everyday. The penny-wise-pound-foolish approach to doing business is common. People often buy automobile insurance on the basis of premiums only and later are surprised and angered when they have a claim and learn what the company will *not* do.

A friend told me his experience with his bargain accountant.

"I used J.J. for six years. I know almost nothing about accounting and I had heard his hourly fees were very low. Then I moved out of state and decided to change accountants. My new accountant charged higher fees, but I was under time pressure so I let him do my returns. He reviewed my statements for the past six years and then told me I simply had been ill-advised. There were no monumental errors, but he said that there were numerous judgmental mistakes covering such matters as depreciation, business expenses, pension and profit-sharing contributions, and withholding taxes. I asked him how much more I had paid in taxes than was required. He replied, 'I can't tell you exactly without a lot of work.

It's too late now to recover what you overpaid because of judgment, but I'm estimating at least one hundred thousand dollars.' "

My friend, over a six-year period, may have saved $4,000 or $5,000 in accounting fees for the privilege of paying $100,000 more in taxes than was required.

Early in my career, I worked for a real penny pincher. One of my duties was to hire clerical personnel. Many times I suggested (but my employer rejected my plan) that we hire the best available people. This would have required a 10 to 20 percent pay premium over "average" personnel. However, my boss favored a low-cost personnel which invariably turned out to be a high-cost one because of its low productivity, mistakes, turnover, and sick days.

BIG THINKERS FOCUS ON LITTLE THINGS, TOO

Harvey S. Firestone said, "Success is the son of detail." How true. Most of us have seen a football game lost because one player did not block the way the play was planned. We've watched comedians flop because their timing was off by a second or less. And we've lost sales because of a wrong inflection in the salesperson's voice when we asked for the order.

Consider this example. Volkswagen is one of the best selling cars ever built. People came to depend on the VW for its endurance and reliability. Detail was important. Then the company started building the car in the United States. Soon, sales fell drastically. And for one reason — attention to detail was ignored. Little things went wrong. Doorknobs fell off. Clutches proved defective. Air conditioners didn't work. Brake systems didn't function properly. Safety problems caused several product recalls.

Volkswagen lost a big share of its market, not because the basic (the big) plan for the car was faulty, but because the detailed instructions on how to put the car together were followed haphazardly. As a result, hundreds of thousands of car buyers ignored VW until credibility was established again.

Lack of attention to detail is in no way only a Volkswagen problem. In some years, more American automobiles are recalled because of carelessness than are manufactured!

A surgeon told me why a knee operation he performed took

five hours instead of three. "The person assigned responsibility for ordering a mechanical part I was to insert into the knee joint ordered the wrong size. It took two hours to get the right part."

More than 100 people died in the crash of an airliner taking off in a snowstorm from Washington National because the pilot figured only a few hundred pounds of ice on the wings wouldn't make a difference. But the extra weight did make a difference and in seconds the plane was in the Potomac.

A big plan combined with detail pays off. Once we have a grand plan worked out, attention to detail pays off. A friend of mine owns two successful restaurants in New Orleans. Each restaurant is a big moneymaker. I asked my friend how he managed to keep his restaurants so busy when most restaurants had a hard time breaking even.

My friend laughed and said, "I have three secrets to explain my success: detail, detail, and detail. Let's start with the menus. The names of every entree, salad, bread, drink, and dessert were selected after painstaking consideration. The decor was chosen only after I had five decorators give me their opinions. I listened to forty violinists play before selecting the three we use. The floral arrangements, furniture, chairs, silver — everything was carefully selected."

"What about the food?" I asked.

"That's the simplest part of the whole operation," my restaurateur friend noted. "We buy only first-quality meats, vegetables, and fruits. So do one hundred restaurants in New Orleans. But the difference is my people pay more attention to details when they prepare the food."

Again, my friend laughed and said, "Detail, detail, and detail."

There you have an example of a restaurant owner who charges about twice as much as his competitors, operates near capacity all the time, and makes a lot of money because he sees the wisdom in the concept "To big thinkers, little things make a huge difference."

A little more attention to detail commands higher prices in everything you do. I asked a clothing manufacturer why he was able to charge 50 to 100 percent more for his suits than his competitors charge.

He replied, "Well, I know you are a big thinker. I am, too. But I am also a little thinker."

"Would you explain?" I asked.

"Glad to."

Then he pulled a suit off the rack and showed me what he did to a suit that cheaper low-price competitors did not do. He showed me the stitching, the weaving, the way the suit was put together, the lining, how the buttons were sewed on — "little" things.

After seeing the demonstration, I understood why he was able to command a larger price.

Perhaps the most significant battle in World War II was the sinking of the German battleship, the "Bismarck." Had the Bismarck not been sunk, Britain would probably have been defeated. So, Churchill absolutely made up his mind the Bismarck must be sunk. In issuing the order to sink the ship, Churchill told his naval commanders over and over and over again to make sure every detail was covered. In a few days, the Bismarck was sunk. Attention to detail made the difference. Attention to "little" things helped Britain survive.

"UNIMPORTANT" THINGS MAKE A BIG DIFFERENCE

As a speaker before trade associations, sales and management seminars, and other groups, I see firsthand several times a week why attention to detail is important.

Here are three oversights I've seen in the last month that detracted from the purpose of a meeting.

Situation 1. An important invited guest's name was misspelled on the program. To those of us who are speaking professionals, having your name misspelled unfortunately goes with the job. My name, Schwartz, has been printed on meeting programs as Swartz, Suarts, Schwarts, Shuarz, and even Schultz.

But to the invited guest, having the last part of his last name spelled *mayer* instead of *meyer* made him furious. He complained angrily to the association's executive director, to its president, and to the staff. Then, when he addressed the group, he made a big deal about his misspelled name. True, he was overreacting. But his anger, even though excessive, underscores a little-but-big point:

Spell people's names correctly — on memos, on letters, on invitations, and on announcements.

An old truism is "A person's name is the most important word in our language."

Situation 2. At an awards banquet where 12 people were to be singled out for extraordinary performances, two people (who had been informed in advance they were to receive an award) were inadvertently left off the presentation list. The oversight went unnoticed for over a week. The people who were overlooked were too reticent to say, "Hey, where's my award?"

But the damage was done. The two people who were not recognized felt left out and unimportant. And their future cooperation and sacrifice was unlikely.

The point: When you're passing out awards, make absolutely certain every person who is supposed to receive one, does.

Situation 3. The Happy Hour runs too long. Happy hours prior to a banquet are an American meeting tradition. Booze flows freely and some attendees take advantage of the opportunity to break previous drinking records. At a recent function, the meeting planner decided to put everyone in a "first-class" mood before the banquet. So, the happy hour was extended from 60 minutes to 90 minutes.

The banquet was attended by about 500 people. When it was time to eat, about a third of them were drunk, another third moderately intoxicated, and the remaining third, sober. Besides allowing the Happy Hour to go on far too long, the meeting planner made another "little" mistake. The bars remained open during dinner so the boozers could order drinks as they ate.

Finally, the speaker, who was a United States senator, spoke. What followed was a disastrous evening. The senator was to make a serious speech. Shortly after he began, several intoxicated people in the audience (who, if sober, would have been polite and minded their manners) began to heckle him. And throughout his talk, at least a dozen people were getting up to go to the restrooms and another dozen were returning after relieving themselves.

Analyze the results: When he finished speaking, the senator was not provoked, he was mad. (He said to me later, "The next time this association or its members want a special favor in Washington, they'll have to find someone else to help them.")

The association leaders were embarrassed. And the sober people in the audience were deeply offended by the behavior of their inebriated compatriots.

The point: Cut the Happy Hour (a small detail) back to no more than 30 minutes. That's enough.

THINK BIG! AVOID ARGUMENTS

Most people argue many times every day. They argue over work assignments and the way to perform them. They argue about where to eat, about politics, and about company affairs. They argue about big things and little things.

But people *never* win arguments.

Here is an amazing fact. You can't win an argument. Argue with your mate over anything — where to go to dinner, vacation plans, or a school for the kids — you lose. A fuss results. And like a bunch of firecrackers tied together, the fuss is like a chain reaction. Before you know it, a seemingly unimportant argument (where to go to dinner) creates many new verbal explosions, ranging from "I can't stand your friends and relatives" to "Why don't you contribute more money to the household?" to "Why do you always have to have your way?"

Argue with a prospective customer about your product's comparative benefits over your competitor's product and you lose. Argue with a traffic cop and an extra violation is added to your ticket. Argue really hard with the umpire or referee and you'll be thrown out of the game, fined or suspended.

When two people argue, each person digs deep into the recesses of his or her mind to prove a point. And the longer people argue about anything, the more convinced each person is that he or she is right. Consider this small and unimportant argument. Bill thinks the Giants' quarterback is the best in the league, but Jack "knows" the Rams have the best quarterback. Bill and Jack go on for an hour, each trying to prove he is right. And the longer they argue, the deeper each probes his memory to prove he is right. From a superficial analysis (which quarterback seems to be the better leader), the argument soon involves percent of passes completed, number of times each quarterback got sacked, scrambling abilities, touchdown passes completed, and on and on.

Now here is the startling conclusion to the argument. Bill is much more certain he is right that the Giants have the better quarterback than before and Jack is far more convinced that the Rams have the best quarterback than before.

Here is a law to remember. The longer and deeper the argument, the more convinced each arguer is that he is right. The art of arguing puts each side on the defensive. And when a person is forced to defend his point of view, the more "evidence" he will dig up to prove why he is right.

Arguments don't change anyone's mind. Presidential debates today are an expected part of the election process. But do the debates, which are formalized arguments adhering to certain ground rules, change people's minds about which candidate they prefer? The pollsters say No. The only good reason for agreeing to debate an opponent in a political campaign is for the candidates to hold on to the support they already have. Refusing to debate the opponent makes one candidate look like a coward and this (not what he says in the debate) may cost him votes. In any David-Goliath situation, most people take the side of David or the underdog.

To focus on the important:

- Put some frosting on the cake. Give people more than they expect. Give more and you'll get more in return.
- To influence people, think "optimum result." Then give them what they visualize as perfect.
- Think quality, not quantity. Remember quality pays while quantity costs in buying merchandise, selecting friends, and making more money.
- Big thinkers focus on details. Keep in mind that "success is the son of detail."

Chapter 4

How to Build Confidence
for Success

The morning after the telecast of a movie about a nuclear holo-caust and how it affected life in a metropolitan area, I asked 100 college students for their reactions. "Did you lose sleep last night worrying about atomic bombs? Did the movie change your mind about nuclear disarmament? Are you really frightened about the possibility of an atomic war?"

The answers were negative. Only three students seemed genuinely concerned or worried about the possibility of a nuclear war and what it would do to our civilization. The possibility of a nuclear war, the most frightful event that could happen, was of little concern.

Following the showing of the nuclear disaster film, there was no increase in the sale of sleeping pills and tranquilizers, nor was there an increase in suicides. Nor were there increases in sales of bomb shelters, canned food, and containers for fresh water.

Conclusion: The most dreadful event that could happen — an event that would literally destroy all that man has accomplished for thousands of years — does not really frighten people!

News item in *The New England Journal of Medicine:* "Over 1,000 people a day die in the United States prematurely because of smok-ers' disease." This is a hard fact. Smoking is the leading cause of early death because it contributes directly to disease of the heart, lungs, kidneys, and bladder and to virtually all other ailments which significantly shorten life.

But are smokers giving up the addiction? A few perhaps. But everyday an estimated 1,100 young people acquire the habit.

Based on the enormous available evidence, it would seem peo-ple would do whatever is necessary to stop smoking. But most smokers reason, "I'll be OK. It may get to other people but not to me," or "I'll quit later," or "I'm still young," or "I know someone who smoked three packs a day and lived to be ninety-two."

Conclusion: Most people who smoke aren't really frightened of what the addiction will do to them.

News item: Alcohol is the second largest cause of premature death. Now how do people react to this danger? Are they really afraid? For the most part, no. Despite enacting tougher drunk driving laws and raising the drinking age, about 25,000 people die each year on highways because of alcohol-related accidents. Another 200,000 will be permanently crippled, and $25 billion in property damage will result. Alcohol-related accidents is the number one killer of people aged 17 to 25, but there is little fear of driving and drinking.

Our real fears — fear of applying for a job, asking for more money, making a sale, doing something our friends disapprove of, getting something we want — are emotionally based. Fears that cripple our initiative and stand between us, success, and the good life have their roots in faulty thinking.

Now here is good news. We can beat these fears. We can enjoy victory over obstacles that keep us from enjoying success, wealth, and happiness.

Let's see how.

TAKE ACTION:
DO WHAT YOU FEAR AND FEAR WILL DISAPPEAR

Mrs. Franklin D. Roosevelt, although the child of a wealthy family, as a young adult was insecure. She felt a severe lack of confidence when she compared herself with her friends. But Eleanor Roosevelt gained great confidence, became a speaker, author, and one of the world's most influential and beloved women of the 20th Century.

How?

Much of Mrs. Roosevelt's triumph over the dread psychological disease, "fear of people," can be traced to her ability to understand how to cure the disease. She wrote in her book *You Learn by Living* —

"You gain strength, courage and confidence by every experience in which you really stop to look fear in the face. You are able to say to yourself, 'I have lived through horror. I can take the next thing that comes along'... you must do the thing you think you cannot do."

In other words, Eleanor Roosevelt beat fear by taking action, by meeting it head on, and by telling herself, "I *can* do and *will* do what I fear."

I share the platform with some of America's greatest speakers. And as we exchange anecdotes and experiences, they admit that even after thousands of presentations each of them still gets butterflies; they still feel uptight and still feel a little scared each time they make a speech. And they agree on something else, too. Feeling a little nervous before a presentation gives the adrenalin a boost, makes them more alert, and encourages them to try even harder to put the message across.

Do the disagreeable task now and reduce worry. Each of us faces tasks we wish would simply disappear. There are many "dreads" in life. Examples are the fear of making a call on a new prospect, the fear of asking for a loan when our credit worthiness is questionable, the fear of applying for a job when the odds are against getting it, the fear of discussing a problem with our spouse, and the fear of making a phone call to discuss a matter with an irate customer.

Here is an important fact: The longer you put off doing the unpleasant, the more unpleasant it becomes. The longer you delay asking for something associated with your job — maybe a pay increase, a transfer, a change in work schedule — the more reasons you will come up with for not asking. Delay enlarges your fear; action eliminates it.

A friend was told by his eye doctor three years ago that he needed a cataract operation. All operations, whether or not life-threatening, are unpleasant. So my friend put it off for three years. Finally, when he was almost blind in one eye, he had the surgery and was back home in six hours. He told me later that the fear of the operation had cost him at least two hours' lost sleep a night for three years — that's well over 2,000 hours. Failure to act also greatly impaired his ability to read, watch TV, and enjoy nature for three years. The do-it-now-if-it's-needed philosophy would have spared my friend all that worry time.

Putting things off strengthens fear; *action eliminates it!*

Do the thing you fear and fear will disappear. Afraid to discuss a problem with your boss? *Discuss it.* Nervous about applying for a job? *Apply for it.* Afraid to ask a person for a date? *Ask for it.*

I asked a friend whose hobby is skydiving how he gained the courage to make that first dive.

"I did two things," he said. "First, I got all the instruction on the ground about how to do it. Second, I jumped."

Procrastination erodes our confidence just as a flood erodes our soil.

You don't want to work for a put-it-off manager. Nor do your people want to work for you if you can't make a decision.

The longer we postpone an unpleasant matter, the longer it worries us and the more pain we endure. Nip a problem in the bud. An untreated sore can become really infected and kill.

HOW TO DEAL WITH "WHAT-WILL-OTHER-PEOPLE-THINK" FEAR

Everyone wants the approval of other people. This is a basic need of human nature. Before doing anything — deciding what to wear, decorating the home, buying a car, or accepting a job — many people ask themselves, "What will my friends say?" "Will they approve?" "Will they laugh and gossip about me behind my back?" Most people fear doing anything they feel may shock, offend, or upset others.

The easy way to deal with the will-other-people-approve? fear (and the method most folks use) is to adhere to strict conformity. But living your life to conform to other people's likes, dislikes, and prejudices stunts your development. Conformists deny themselves individuality, an ingredient you must have to enjoy success.

Here are two suggestions to beat the do-other-people-approve? fear:

> 1. If what you want to do meets moral and legal standards, *do it!* Your life is your life. Friends who criticize what you do aren't really friends. Chances are the people

who think your behavior should always meet their standards won't be there when you need money, a job, or help.
And the folks who want you to think and act the way
they do would delight in seeing you fail or get into some
kind of trouble. Remember this: People who expect you
to conform to their way of viewing things are themselves
very insecure.

2. Seek the approval of people you admire most. Select
a mentor. Instead of asking, "What will other people
think?" ask, "Would the most successful person I know
approve of what I have in mind?" Think and do as successful people think and do.

DEFEAT FEAR WITH PREPARATION

Every four years, the public is treated to a televised debate between the two major candidates for President of the United States.
One hundred million or more people watch. The candidate who
is behind in the polls wants to catch up; the one who is ahead
tries to protect his lead. Millions of votes and quite possibly the
election depend on which candidate appears to better understand
the nation's challenges and has the better solutions for these
problems.

And make no mistake. Each candidate is nervous, afraid. Months
and even years of campaigning are on the line. Each candidate
is concerned about the hard work of volunteers, financial contributions, and, above all, the welfare of the nation.

Neither candidate knows exactly what questions will be asked.
But they know the general areas that will be covered, such as economic issues, foreign trade, national defense, and social welfare.

For a few days prior to the debate, each candidate typically fore-
goes campaigning, goes into seclusion, and prepares. A staff member will play the role of the opposing candidate. Other campaign
staffers will play the role of reporters and ask questions they an-
ticipate will be asked by the press during the actual debate. This
elaborate acting-out of the debate has one purpose — to prepare
the candidate for the best possible performance by giving him confidence. The public senses immediately as they watch the candidates

who is the more confident. And the public wants a President who is strong, confident, assured and, at the same time, humble. The voters want a person who has knowledge of the issues. Note what Emerson wrote — "Fear always springs from ignorance." And voters do not support a candidate who is unprepared because of ignorance. Incomplete and inadequate knowledge is a prime cause of fear.

Preparation helps defeat fear. Winning prizefighters prepare for a bout by selecting a sparring partner who has a boxing style similar to their opponent.

A football coach helps defeat fear and builds team confidence through exhaustive preparation. Films of the other opposing team in action are reviewed, "special" plays are practiced over and over again, and restrictions are placed on players' activities all because, in an even contest, confidence is the deciding factor and confidence comes from preparation.

Preparation builds confidence on job interviews. Interviewers tell me most people applying for a job, whether teenagers, recent college graduates, or people in their middle years, show fear when being interviewed for a job. Some people are so afraid they can't look the interviewer in the eyes, have lapses in memory, squirm in their chair, and perspire profusely.

Why? The major reason for this fear is lack of knowledge. A friend in the personnel placement business told me what kind of preparation is needed to beat interview fear.

- Know the kind of work you seek — the ins and outs of the job.
- Know how your ability, your personality, and your desire match the job. Know why you are qualified and why you want the job.
- Know the company offering the job — what does it do? How is it performing? Problems it may be undergoing?

The more you know about a company and the job you seek, the more confident you appear. And the more confident you are, the better your chances of getting the job you want.

How to gain confidence in selling. Next to public speaking, more people are afraid of selling than any other occupation. And again, preparation is a key to overcoming the near paralysis people have in making a sales presentation. People fear looking stupid, hearing the prospect say "No," being embarrassed, forgetting what they want to say about the product, asking for the order, and not making the sale.

A good friend of mine, John Evans, is a world class sales trainer. "The bottom line in selling," John explained, "is preparation. A salesperson should possess humility. He or she should be emphatic. But to sell, a person must display confidence — 'I am totally convinced what I offer you meets your needs.'

"Now," John went on, "the best way — in fact, the only way — to gain the high-level confidence needed to sell successfully is preparation. And preparation is knowledge — knowledge of what you sell, knowledge of how your product will help the prospect or client, and knowledge of the person you're selling.

"Know your product or service. Know exactly what it can do for the prospect. Be so well prepared you can answer any question that comes up. Know construction, desirability, guarantees. Know the limitations, when not to use the product.

"Second, know how your product or service will help your prospect. Your customer is the law of self-interest in action. As a salesman makes a presentation, the customer is asking, 'How does this relate to my problem? How would it benefit me?'

"The third confidence builder is knowledge of the prospect. You don't sell to machines, you sell only to people. Just as you feel confident and have no fear when you're around people you know well, you'll have confidence around prospects when you know more about their personal interests, personality, personal responsibilities, job responsibilities, and family.

"So, to act confidently in a sales situation, prepare yourself with knowledge of what you sell, how it will benefit the prospect, and who the prospect is.

"But more than knowledge is required to gain confidence needed in selling. And that is practice, practice, and practice. Practice your presentation with people who act the role of a customer. Practice before a mirror, or better yet, film yourself on a TV camera. Watch your mannerisms, listen to your voice, observe your expressions."

You'll destroy fear and build confidence in selling through preparation. In any activity, confidence comes in direct proportion to preparation.

GET SPECIALIZED KNOWLEDGE

For generations, most people never sought specialized knowledge after completing school. What they learned about business, managing, selling, or their profession was acquired on an accidental hit-or-miss basis.

Now that's changed. Today there are seminars, clinics, short courses, and conferences where you can learn the latest techniques and knowledge about anything you need to know. These sources of specialized knowledge have three advantages over conventional education. They are taught by experts, not by people whose only qualification is a degree. Second, the subject matter relates directly to your needs. Irrelevant information is avoided. And third, you'll acquire as much useful information from other attendees as you do from the instructors. Specialized learning meetings attract only sharp people eager to make more money and enjoy greater success.

PROGRAM YOUR PERSONAL MEMORY COMPUTER TO RETRIEVE ENCOURAGING INFORMATION

Everything that has happened to each of us is stored in our memory. Memory is to our mind what storage is to a computer. There are virtually tens of billions of events in your memory bank waiting for the conscious you to retrieve them. Specific details of childhood discipline, associations with other children, day-by-day events in school, all your interactions with people — everything that has ever happened to you or involved you is in your mental storage vault.

Your memory is an amazing place! Every one of the billions of things you have seen, conversations you have heard, objects you have touched, odors you have smelled, and food and liquids you have tasted (all your physical senses have ever experienced) are in your memory. And more. Your spiritual sensations, your thoughts, and your feelings are also in your mind. The conscious mind is unaware of all that is stored in your memory vault. But your subconscious mind is. Yet, the working of your subconscious mind is controlled by your conscious thinking.

You may consciously remember only a very small share of the events that have shaped you into the person you are today. But your subconscious mind remembers them all and directly affects your behavior.

You are the only person who can access your mental storage bank to your advantage. When fear seems to gain hold of your thoughts, when your confidence slips, when you feel your world is coming apart, you have two choices:

(1) You can recall the negative, depressing, discouraging thoughts of the past and let them be the mental food you consume, or

(2) You can recall happy thoughts, moments of victory, your assets.

What you call up from your memory bank is critically important. Call up the negatives and you'll find even more reasons why you "won't make it," why you'll lose next time you try. Bad memories, failure memories, defeat memories simply reinforce your present situation.

Recall the many times you tried but failed; remember the advice you've received telling you your ideas are foolish and your goals too high; relive the embarrassing moments you've experienced and your fear will beat you.

Or you can exercise the positive option. You can tell your memory bank to withdraw good nourishing thoughts from your memory storage vault. You can pull up victories, successes, wholesome experiences that enrich you and refuel your confidence. Recall words of encouragement you've received, admiration others have expressed for you, your achievements, and your accomplishments.

You see, your memory bank doesn't care which set of thoughts you withdraw. It is simply a repository of your life's events. *You* are the decider; the memory bank has no prejudices. The conscious part of your thinking apparatus decides whether to withdraw successful thoughts and beat fear, or withdraw failure thoughts and let fear beat you.

Let's say you are facing an important interview. You need the cooperation of the person you will meet. But you're scared. You are afraid you'll lose. Now, if you recall memories, such as "remember how poor your grades were in school, you got laughed at because of language mistakes, you don't have all the necessary skills, your former spouse thought you were a fool," your confidence will be destroyed.

But if you program your mental computer to pull up good confidence-building memories (friendships, past successes, games you won, jobs you've held, all the successes that made you the person you are), your confidence will grow.

ACCEPT RISKS — THEY ARE BUILDING BLOCKS OF SUCCESS

A person's confidence is best measured by his or her willingness to take risks. Fear is best reflected by the degree to which a person seeks to avoid risk.

The old saying "Nothing ventured, nothing gained" will always be true. Risk, the possibility of loss, is as necessary to success as air is to life.

Imagine what would happen if everyone decided to try to live 100 percent risk-free:

> • No farmer would plant a crop because there might be too much rain or too little. Or the market price for the grain might collapse.
>
> • No one would start a business because competition might cause it to fail.
>
> • No television programs would be produced because there might be too few viewers to attract advertisers.
>
> • Investors would not put money into new construction, into oil well exploration, and into new ventures.
>
> • Artists and authors would stop work because people might reject their creativity.

To be completely secure, people would take their money out of banks (the banks may fail), hoard food (there may be an atomic war), refuse to drive cars (I may have an accident), and patients in hospitals would refuse blood transfusions (the blood may be contaminated). A goal of 100 percent security would almost overnight destroy our economy.

To avoid risk completely, no one would apply for a job (you may not get it), submit a poem to a literary journal (it may be rejected), ask a friend for a date (you may be turned down), speak up in a meeting (you may be laughed at), or ask for an order (the prospect may say No).

Here is an important point: Success-oriented people take risks and sometimes the risks turn out to be losses. Thirty-seven percent of today's millionaires went broke after accumulating wealth. But they came back to win. No investor is always "right," and people who build shopping centers, residential neighborhoods, and office buildings sometimes lose money. In the oil drilling business, a majority of wells turn out to be dry holes.

No football coach has a perfect season every year. All musicians make mistakes.

How we react to defeat is the key. You have heard people who have failed in a job or in a business of their own say, "I've had it. Never again!"

At times, we all feel like giving up. And if we're not careful, we will give up. Pressure from peers to surrender can be powerful. They tell you, "Look, you tried. The plan didn't work. Why beat your head against a wall? Don't feel bad. Most people who try something new fail."

These people — your peers and "friends" — are often glad to see you surrender. It's disappointing but it's true. They don't have the courage to do something on their own. If they see you fail, they feel better about themselves; you are one of them — another mediocrity.

HOW TO WIN CONFIDENCE IN ONE-ON-ONE SITUATIONS

Most often, what you want is gained or lost in one-on-one situations. Typically, when you apply for a job, it is you versus one other person who has the power to say Yes or No. If you sell, usually you make your presentation to one person who again has the power to make a yes-or-no decision. And when you have a performance evaluation, request a promotion, or want something special, you usually talk to only one person who represents power and authority.

To add to your fear, the person you are to meet has the home court advantage. You make your sales presentation in your prospect's office, not yours. You talk to your boss in his or her quarters, not your own. It's natural to feel a little intimidated because the person you want to influence is in a familar environment and you are not.

Tonight, in thousands of homes, one spouse is saying to the other, "You seem uptight — what's bothering you?" The reply: "My performance review is tomorrow and I'm nervous," or "The department head wants to see me tomorrow, and I'm worried because I don't know what he or she wants," or "I'm calling on a new prospect tomorrow. I hear he is a tough character."

Some people have extreme problems with one-on-one encounters. We may experience dread and apprehension *before* the conversation, nervousness and fear *during* the discussion, and regret *afterwards* because we feel we didn't make our point and goofed.

Often people fail miserably in conversations with an authority figure. Little Jimmy, called to the principal's office for being 30 minutes late everyday for a week is so frightened he can't explain that he had to babysit his little sister because his mother's work schedule was changed.

Betty is terribly nervous in a job interview and fails to mention some important work experiences. And Bill who has some sound ideas on how to run the company better feels threatened by Mr. Big Boss. When asked for his suggestions, he forgets his ideas.

Keep in mind that some managers and other people in authority take courses to learn how to intimidate other people. Shameful as teaching people how to bully others is, we must recognize the practice exists.

How then do we deal with authority figures when we lack confidence? How do we get the confidence to present our ideas to another person who can say "Yes" or "No?" Here are two suggestions that will work for you:

1. *Tell yourself before the meeting, "We are two important people sitting down to discuss something of mutual importance."* I need what the other person has to offer. But he or she needs what I have to offer. The discussion affects both of our destinies. Concentrate on common goals.

When we were young, we were taught to respect adults, teachers, and others in authority. Such teaching is good. Authority must be respected to make any social organization, whether it be a family or a huge business, work.

In learning to respect authority, however, many people are taught to fear it, not respect it.

Respect people in authority, YES. Fear people in authority, NO.

Fear of authority and the lack of confidence it creates is a real barrier to success. So, as you prepare for the interview, repeat to yourself, "We are two important people about to discuss something of mutual importance."

2. *Remind yourself the other person is a human being, not God.* He or she digests food, breathes, and coughs the same way you do. The person may be poised and important. But he or she is still a human creature with worries, frustrations, problem children, spouse problems, money problems, and concern that other people are beating him or her in the corporate game. And keep in mind that the person in authority may be just as afraid of you as you are of him or her. The person buying what you sell is afraid of making a mistake and looking bad to his superior. And the manager you report to is always concerned about what the manager he reports to will think of him. It is unfortunate but true that people at all organizational levels run scared. We're more alike than we are different.

PROJECT THE "I'M-CONFIDENT" LOOK

Do a little research with a close friend. Say something as, "You and Charles are so close. May I ask how you became attracted to each other?"

Your friend will probably say something, such as "Oh, we found we had so many common interests it was only natural we wanted to be together."

Or say to a man, "You and Sonya seem so compatible. What brought you together?" And the possible response is, "I met her at a party. Soon we discovered we both liked tennis and shared common goals. First thing I knew, we were married."

Now both of your friends gave good reasons for selecting their mates. But each of them "overlooked" that appearance — a mutual physical attraction — was there before the common interests were discovered.

Appearance *does* determine attractiveness. Appearance is a dominant factor in selecting a mate.

A sure way to gain confidence and overcome fear is to develop a confident look. When you know you look confident, you feel confident and project confidence. Other people will immediately sense this and show greater respect for you.

Product or package appearance is an enormously important marketing activity. Companies spend more than $200 billion a year on product and package design to give appeal to what they sell. In buying a car, many people never look at the engine; it's design that counts. In buying food, most folks never look at the ingredients; it's the label that does the convincing.

And in deciding whether to offer you a job, to ask you for a date, or to purchase your products, your appearance subconsciously affects their decision.

People *do* judge a book by its cover. A person may change her opinion about the book if she opens it and reads a few pages. But unless she knows the author, she is not likely to even bother to open the book if the cover — the package — is not inviting.

Dressing right for the situation makes you more salable. People judge you by the way you look. Here is what happens:

- People evaluate your ideas by your look of expertise.
- Your employees or support people react positively when you project the look of authority.
- Customers and clients like to do business with you when you look prosperous.
- Bankers will loan you money when you look like you don't need it!

Just as people approve or disapprove of food, cars, and houses by the way they look, they make up their minds about you by the way you look.

REMEMBER, 90 PERCENT OF YOU IS PACKAGED

At work or in public, people see only about ten percent of the naked you — your head, face, neck, and hands. Ninety percent of a man is packaged under a suit, shirt, socks, and shoes. And about 90 percent of a woman is covered by a dress, blouse, suit, stockings, and shoes.

The way people package themselves directly affects one's attitudes toward himself or herself (I like me or I don't like me). Our packaging also determines other people's attitudes toward us. "That person looks great so he or she must be great," or, at the other extreme, "That person looks like a slob, so he or she must be a slob."

Proper personal packaging benefits you two ways. First, you become more confident, more at ease with people, better able to deal with new situations. The right packaging gives you inner strength.

Second, looking great immediately gives you a winning edge. People want to do business with you when you look attractive and successful.

Question: "When do I know I'm dressed right for the situation?"

Answer: "When you feel so comfortable with your appearance you don't ask yourself or other people, 'Do I look OK?' You're dressed suitably when you can concentrate fully on the task at hand and not think about the way you are 'packaged'. "

I heard a sales manager give this advice to his sales force: "Dress so appropriately for the situation that you consciously forget what you're wearing. Your job is to concentrate one hundred percent on the client's needs and how you can satisfy them. If you're worried about the way you look, some of your mental energy is misdirected."

WHAT ABOUT THE 10 PERCENT OF YOU YOU DON'T COVER UP?

What does the part of you that can't be packaged — your face and your eyes have to do with confidence? Let me explain.

A sure way to project confidence is smile and smile and smile. Try this: Project a real smile and try to be afraid of someone or something. You can't. Nor can you worry or be angry!

I've been close to Charles W. for 25 years. He is a successful entrepreneur in the printing business and he is a smiler. When "impossible" deadlines come up, Charles smiles. In the middle of bidding on a big contract, Charlie is smiling. When employees are uptight about a problem, Charlie just keeps on smiling.

Once I complimented Charlie on his habit of smiling all the time even when most people would see nothing to smile about. Charlie, smiling, of course, thanked me and said, "I taught myself to smile regardless of what's happening. It makes me feel better. And it disarms other people. They may come to me upset or mad or worried. But my smile always puts them in a better mood."

HOW TO USE YOUR EYES TO WIN ACCEPTANCE

Your eyes can help you in two ways: First, looking other people in the eye says to them, "I'm confident," "I'm a winner," and "I know what I'm doing." If you don't look the other person in the eye when you make a statement or make a request, the other person will assume you're hiding something, you're not being honest, or you're weak and afraid.

If you are a timid person, there is only one way to get the eye-contact habit. Practice looking people in the eye until it is second nature.

But there is much more to using your eyes to win acceptance than just looking in another person's eyes. What your eyes say is what determines the most important reaction of other people to you. The eyes truly are the mirror of the soul. Eyes always tell the truth about how you feel. At any moment, one's eyes can express love, disgust, hate, fear, or whatever emotion one feels.

A similar experiment will illustrate this. Select a friend to help you discover the revealing power of your eyes. Look at your friend and for two or three seconds think deeply and sincerely, "I love you." Then ask your friend, "What did my eyes say?" Your friend may say, "Your eyes said you like or love me." Then without changing your facial expression, look at your friend with hate and anger in your mind. Again, ask your friend, "What did my eyes say?" And the other person will respond, "Your eyes said you don't like me."

Your eyes reflect every emotion you feel — love, hate, contempt, joy, fear, worry.

Understand and practice this point. To convey an expression in your eyes, *you must think the expression in your mind.* You must *think* "I care about you" for your eyes to say "I care about you."

Remember, your eyes are a picture of your soul. *No* one, absolutely no one, can change the image his or her eyes project without first changing the way he or she thinks. Only a second or two may be needed to change a thought — and what the eyes say. But the process is fixed, always true.

You can use this attitude projection technique in important encounters with other people. Imagine this situation: You don't like your boss but you need a special favor from him. Before you make your request, think of several things about the person you do admire (perhaps hard work, how the person overcomes obstacles, loyalty to staff, or knowledge). Think about something you can admire and you've greatly improved your chances for a successful request.

THINK OF A LOSS AS A LESSON

Today space travel is so routine it barely makes the news. Yet more than 16,000 space vehicles were launched before a man was put into earth orbit. Each failure was analyzed to answer two questions: "What went wrong?" and "How can we correct the problem in the next launch?"

Air travel is by far the safest mode of transportation today because every air disaster or "defeat" is studied to learn why the crash occurred and how it can be prevented. In World War II, the United States lost 33,000 airplanes. Because we were at war, not each crash could be analyzed in detail. But airplanes were made much safer because of what we did learn. Air travel is now so safe that there is only one fatality per 100 billion miles flown. How safe is commercial flying? One would need to fly 600 miles per hour 24 hours a day for more than 1,000 years to meet the probability of death in an aircraft accident. The danger today is not the flight, but the trip to and from the airport. The highway trip is 1,562 times as likely to result in a death as is a trip made in flight!

Advances in medicine result because physicians regard a loss as a lesson. A generation ago a heart by-pass operation was so risky it was only a last-resort procedure. Now, because surgeons have learned from past losses, some doctors perform several such operations a day!

A fire is an unfortunate tragic event. But when fire inspectors find the cause, building codes are written to prevent a similar incident.

Think of the most successful people you know. Each of them "lost" far more often than they "won." Probe, and you'll discover every prominent person has endured setbacks such as hearing "no" more often than "yes," being turned down for a job, getting fired from a job, being in accidents, enduring bad health, suffering drug addiction, making miserable investments, and undergoing humiliation.

The secret to success is not avoidance of defeat; rather, it is growth through defeat. A loss is always a potential lesson. No child has yet learned to walk without stumbling, staggering, and falling dozens of times in the process. Every great entertainer has botched many performances before becoming consistently good. And every admired manager has made dozens of bad mistakes.

The point: Everyone makes mistakes. How we choose (notice I use the word *choose*) to view losses, defeats, and errors ultimately determines who succeeds and who lives in mediocrity.

Our very best effort is expected from all professionals. Everything we do deserves our best effort. But perfection is unattainable. Defeats will always occur. No plan, no machine, no enterprise of any kind will ever be absolutely fail-safe. Losses are inevitable. The big question is, "Do we learn from the loss?"

A key to success and winning confidence is the post-mortem. If we're smart, after a defeat we ask two questions:

1. *What went wrong?* Remember, every defeat has an explanation.
2. *How can I correct what went wrong?* There are always new approaches to any problem.

FOR DEEP-DOWN CONFIDENCE, PUT THESE CONCEPTS TO WORK:

- Recognize the roots of fear — mismanaged thinking.
- Do what you fear and fear will disappear.

- Build confidence with preparation. Overcome fear of job interviews, sales presentations, and loan requests with a get-ready-for-it program.
- Tap your mind for victory memories, never defeat memories. Remember, only you can control your thoughts.
- If what you want to do is moral and legal, *do* it!
- To win in one-on-one situations, a) tell yourself, "We are two important people discussing something of mutual importance" and b) remind yourself that the other person is also a human being.
- Develop the confident look. Package yourself so other people are interested in you.
- Give your eyes the right kind of power by thinking good, positive thoughts.
- A loss is a lesson. Learn it and proceed to greater success.

Chapter 5

Give 100% for Success

There is little getting without a whole lot of giving. Generosity ("What can I give the other person?"), not selfishness ("What can the other person give me?"), leads to success, wealth, and happiness. The more you give, the more you get. Successful people are generous. And they give more of themselves than is expected.

Concentrate on giving, and getting soon becomes automatic. Let's see how.

THINK: A DOZEN IS REALLY THIRTEEN

When I was a small boy, my father sold sweet corn (we called them roasting ears) to people who lived in a nearby small town. Soon after I was able to count, my father assigned the responsibility to me of putting the ears of corn in neat stacks of one dozen ears. That made me feel very proud because, even though only five years old, I felt I was making a contribution. So, as instructed, I made stacks of corn, each with exactly 12 ears.

Then, when my dad reviewed a few samples of my counting, he went to a basket, got some more ears of corn and added one ear to each stack. This made me angry and I said to my father, "I know how to count. A dozen means twelve. Now each stack is thirteen ears. Thirteen is not a dozen," I protested. (My dad's action also irritated me because each ear sold for a penny and to me a penny was a lot of money.)

My father, smiling, gently explained, "When we sell sweet corn, every dozen is thirteen ears. You see, we sell only good corn. But with the husks still on the ear, there might just be a bad ear we don't know about. So we give our friends an extra ear. We never want our customers to feel cheated.

"Also," Dad continued, "we want everyone who buys our corn to tell their neighbors in town how good our roasting ears are. That way, we will sell more corn and make more money."

I saw other examples of people giving a liberal count in selling their products. On the farm we bought baby chicks from a hatchery hundreds of miles away. The hatchery would send them by mail in boxes containing 100 chicks.

When the chicks arrived, it was my job to count them. And always there were 107 or 108 chicks — not the 100 we had ordered. It was the hatchery's way of saying it put some extra chicks in the box just in case a few of them might be sick. This practice by the hatchery was a wonderful — and a smart — way to keep customers, to avoid negative correspondence, and to build its business.

Years later, of course, I learned that "a-dozen-is-13" concept had long been practiced by some bakers — hence, the term "baker's dozen." But by then, giving an extra measure was already part of my nature.

Give a little extra and you are a hero. Give less than is expected and you put yourself on someone's "hate list." Everyone, yes everyone, likes to get more than they bargained for. No one, absolutely no one, likes to be cheated. Getting less than you pay for makes you angry, hurts your ego, and makes you want to bad-mouth the business that took advantage of you.

SMART PEOPLE ADD TO — FOOLISH PEOPLE TAKE AWAY

The most important way we learn is by thoughtful observation. Lessons that teach us success fundamentals are available in every encounter with other people.

Consider this example. You visit a candy store and order a pound of unboxed candy. The person behind the counter puts a big scoop of candy on the scales, maybe 20 ounces, and then begins to take away your candy, piece by piece, until the weight is exactly 16 ounces.

How do you feel? Cheated. Subconsciously, you perceived the big 20-ounce pile of candy as *your* candy. Now, as the person behind the counter takes some of it away, you feel *your* candy is being stolen.

Intelligent people behind the counter use the add-to approach. They put a relatively small amount of candy on the scales, maybe 10 or 12 ounces. Then, they add a few pieces until the scale shows 16 ounces. Subconsciously, this makes you feel good because you perceive you are getting extra candy.

Sixteen ounces is still 16 ounces. But the way a pound is counted makes a mighty big difference. Recently, a woman ahead of me at the seafood counter in a supermarket ordered a pound of shrimp. The store person carelessly put almost two pounds on the scale and then began to take the surplus shrimp away. Finally, when he had reduced the pile to 16 ounces, the lady said, with anger in her voice, "I've changed my mind. I don't want them," and walked away.

To be sure, counter personnel must be careful in weighing merchandise. Shrimp that day were $14 a pound — that's 87½ cents per ounce. But the point is *never* make the customer feel cheated.

Successful businesses search for creative ways to use the generous add-on tactic to increase sales. The magazine subscription that includes a free pocket calculator, a remote-control device that comes free with the purchase of a television set, and the two-for-the-price-of-one sale by a drug chain are examples. People like you and buy from you when you give more than they expect in exchange for their money.

Evidence that generosity, the add-on approach, works wonders is overwhelming. Nevertheless, there are still many businesses that believe success is spelled CHEAT. Stores that advertise non-existent appliances at a ridiculously low price and then try to browbeat and intimidate the customer into buying a much higher priced product are common examples. Observe such scoundrels only to learn how *not* to succeed.

You can use the "add-to" principle in every facet of life.

- Give unexpected, extra service to your employer and you become a candidate for more pay, for more fringe benefits, and for promotion.
- Put something extra into your assignment at school and get a better grade.

- Give more time to your kids and get more love and cooperation in return.
- Show respect to the parking lot attendant and your car gets better treatment.

WHEN YOU'VE MOWED THE LAWN, TRIM THE SHRUBS

In many organizations we find job specialists — people who set the standards for the amount and quality of work a person doing a specific task is expected to accomplish in a given amount of time. Over a period of time, a person becomes conditioned to what he or she is expected to do — not what the person can and wants to do. Unfortunately, we have become a do-the-bare-minimum-required society, not a give-it-a-100-percent-maximum-effort nation. Rarely are people encouraged by the promise of more money or other incentives to do more than the minimum required. And if some person does volunteer for additional tasks after completing his or her regular assignment, co-workers may scoff.

Much of the haggling of union leaders in contract negotiations is over how *little* their members must do. A union executive takes pride (evil as it is) in telling members, "Look, I got you more pay for doing less. Give me your vote, more money, an unlimited expense account, and a chauffered limousine, and next time we negotiate I'll get you even more for doing less. And I'll go to Washington and tell those people to save your jobs."

Right there is a big chunk of the nation's productivity and trade problem. Workers in other nations are encouraged to do more; here, workers are given all possible incentives to do less.

As a child growing up on a farm, I remember there was no standard unit of work. The first assigned task one day might be "mow the lawn" (and without the benefit of a power mower). And the primary task was always followed with a secondary task — "then trim the shrubs." Or a primary task might be "get the fence repaired," followed by a secondary task — "get started chopping the weeds."

There was never an artificial standard spelling out what constituted "enough" work. There was always more to do than time to do it. And since the work was necessary and varied, it was fun.

Here is a basic principle for moving ahead on the job, winning promotions, making more money and, most important, enjoying work: Do the assigned task as efficiently and quickly as possible and then volunteer to do more. Remember, "when you've mowed the lawn, trim the shrubs."

Let me give you an example of a very successful person who made his way to the top by volunteering. Four weeks ago, I was in California's famed Silicon Valley to talk to the management group of a leading computer company. During dinner and prior to making my talk, I said to my host, "You mentioned that the Chief Executive Officer would be here. Where is he?"

My friend said, "He's seated at the third table on your left."

I glanced at the table, saw no one who looked like a CEO and resumed my conversation with my host. After a few minutes, I again asked my host, "Where is the CEO seated?" My host again indicated the table and described the person who was the CEO.

"That fellow?" I said. "Why, he can't be thirty-five. Is he really the CEO?"

My host laughed and said, "He is only thirty-four and he is the CEO. Tim (the CEO) joined us thirteen years ago fresh out of college where he studied computer science. He was assigned to me. The first job I gave him was auditing our billing procedures. We sell our computer systems to big hospitals. I didn't think anything was wrong, but work was temporarily short and I mainly wanted to give Tim something to do to get his feet wet.

"In two days, Tim came to me and said, 'I've found a problem in the program, but we can correct it easily.' I had not suspected a problem but Tim found one that was costing us over thirty thousand dollars a month. Now, I had thought inspecting the billing program would have kept Tim busy for at least a month. But in only two days he found a problem we didn't suspect and saved us a lot of money.

"Then Tim came to me and said, 'What's next, chief?' That's been Tim since the beginning. He tackled dozens of complex problems, solved them in record time, and kept asking for more to do.

"Tim moved up fast. In four years, I was reporting to him instead of the other way around. He kept mastering his assigned task and then looked for more to do. When it came time to appoint a new CEO, he was the unanimous choice of the Board and the key executives he would manage."

For a moment my mind went back to the time I was told, "When you've mowed the lawn, trim the shrubs." The philosophy works!

Consider this observation: You and I, try as hard as we can, cannot control the destiny of the economy. But you and I can control our own economic destinies. Regardless of the condition of the overall economy, we can enjoy great prosperity, happiness, and peace of mind. A key part of success is volunteering to do more. Give all we've got to the task at hand and then ask to do more.

Tip to managers: Give your people a reward system based on performance and watch your people do more than you dream is possible.

JIMMY O. QUIT SCHOOL AND IS MAKING IT BECAUSE HE GIVES A BEST EFFORT

About the biggest disgrace to parents these days is for a child to drop out of school. A drop-out to most of us is about the worst thing that can happen. "High school drop-out" in the American culture means unemployment, crime, delinquency, drugs, and a wasted life. Parents and educators assume: a) all kids should go to school until they have at least finished high school (some set a minimum of two years in junior college); b) time spent in school is always good for the young person; and c) a young person can't make a living if he or she drops out.

This sort of generalizing is bad for a lot of young people and it's bad for society, too.

Advocates of keep-kids-in-school-regardless-of-what-it-does-to-them cannot take pride in maintaining guards in hallways and requiring students to pass through airport-like metal detectors.

The plain truth is, some young people *should* drop out of school in their early teens. A social responsibility should be to provide opportunities for young people who don't respond to formal education. Forcing a young person to stay in school when he or she doesn't want to often creates boredom, frustration, and an urge to rebel. These are the forces that help push a kid into crime, drugs, and other troubles.

Let me tell you about Jimmy O., a young person I know who

dropped out of school and is doing very well — far better than some of his peers who, too, don't want to stay in school but are pressured into doing so.

I met Jimmy O. four years ago. I answered the doorbell one cool December morning and there was this kid. He looked about 14, stood maybe 5' 5", and was skinny as a twig. He said, "Good morning," very politely, "I'm looking for work. I noticed that you have a bunch of logs in your back yard that are too big to fit in your fireplaces. Let me cut them to the right size so if it gets really cold, you'll have plenty of fireplace wood."

I told the young fellow, "That makes sense, but I don't have an ax or a wedge."

"No problem," he said, "I brought my own." Then I noticed his bicyclc and, sure enough, he had an ax and a wedge neatly tied to the frame. (Notice he had anticipated doing business with me. Anyone selling anything should assume he'll get the order.)

"How much do you charge?" I asked.

"Five dollars per hour," he replied.

"But that's well above the minimum wage," I responded.

"I know," he said, "but I work! I'll give you my best effort."

The youngster emphasized the word work so strongly, I decided to let him go ahead and split the logs. In my mind, I knew the kid wasn't worth the money, but I liked him and figured the extra money I was going to pay him was like a contribution to a worthy cause.

He proceeded to cut the logs and I went to my office. I figured the log chopping would take at least four hours, but in less than two hours he was ringing the bell to my office.

"Dr. Schwartz," Jimmy said, "I'm finished chopping and stacking the wood. How about letting me clean out your boat harbor?"

I was amazed at how quickly he had chopped the wood, so I said, "Go ahead."

Over the next five years, Jimmy did all sorts of jobs for me inside and outside the house. At the same time, he was building a clientele in the neighborhood doing chores few want to do these days — cleaning out gutters, washing walls, carrying off trash, and mowing the lawn.

One day, I asked Jimmy why he wasn't going to school. Very

candidly, he explained, "I was plain bored with the stuff they were trying to teach me because it wasn't doing me any good. You see, I like to work with my hands; I like variety, and I want to be my own boss. Besides, my grandmother and I are alone and she's not well, so making money is especially important to me. I give half of what I earn to her and save most of the other half."

Jimmy O. is now 19 and is still working for me. He now has two assistants, aged 16, a truck, and lawnmowers and other tools needed to serve his ever-expanding clientele.

As I watch Jimmy's business grow, I often reflect on how fortunate everyone is because he dropped out of school to do what he wanted to do and what needs to be done. Jimmy doesn't have to worry about "making it" in this "cruel" world. Jimmy *is* making it. Forcing him to stay in school and learn algebra (which he didn't like), know why the Roman Empire fell (something else that didn't interest him), study factors that led to the War between the States (something nobody agrees on), and wade through how an atom is structured (physics really bored him) would have encouraged him to negative escape — drugs, possibly delinquency, or worse. But Jimmy had the courage to find his place in life and is happy because of it.

Often, Jimmy and I talk. And I'm amazed at the penetrating questions he wants to discuss, such as "What's really wrong with the tax system?" "Are import quotas a good idea?" and "How can I best invest my money?"

And Jimmy has big goals. For years he had told me that someday he wants to own a place where motorcyclists can test their skills and enjoy bike riding. Well, last week he told me he has made a down payment on 100 acres fifty miles from the city which he will develop into a "motorcycle haven." And Jimmy has just turned 19. He'll be a millionaire before he's 30.

Truly, Jimmy has something to give and he's giving it!

Granted, in the emerging new age we will need highly trained engineers, architects, physicians, computer experts, and scientists. But not everyone is cut out for these activities. Forcing people to perform work that doesn't challenge them is more than foolish; it is also cruel, short-sighted, and counter-productive.

FOUR GIFTS THAT GET POWERFUL RESULTS

A good gift comes from your heart. It says, "I think and care about you. I am your friend." Unless the gift uplifts and reassures another person, it has no real lasting impact. Worse still, it is not appreciated.

It's thought value, not monetary value, that makes a gift great. Just as love cannot be bought with money, love cannot be given with money.

GIVE A MORALE-BOOSTING PHONE CALL

Next to a face-to-face conversation, a phone call is the most personal way to communicate. Thinking of a phone call as a gift to convey hope, to offer congratulations for a job well done, and to inspire people to keep up their good work, is a powerful way to deepen a friendship.

The president of a manufactured housing company told me how he uses the telephone as a gift to help keep his 300 dealers enthusiastic.

"I set aside all day every Wednesday to call fifty to sixty dealers. I don't call them to discuss marketing strategy or to review their performance. We have eight sales managers who do that. My calls are strictly goodwill. I let each dealer know I'm proud of him, inquire about his family, his health, those sorts of things. I'll call most dealers seven or eight times a year. It's a great way to put some spirit into our business."

Practice giving phone calls. The phone is a convenient way to congratulate people for an achievement. And it's a great way to let another person know you feel he or she is important because it is unexpected.

So, if someone you know gets promoted, changes jobs, has a child, or gets an award — give him a call. That someone will remember you for a long time.

GIVE THE GIFT OF YOUR TIME

Children whose parents never seem to have time for them wonder, even at a very young age, "Why does Dad or Mom always find time to work or to go to a party or a meeting but not to have time for me?" or "Other kids' parents watch the Little League game, but my Dad just drops me off and picks me up when the game is over," or "When my Dad does talk to me, it seems he's thinking about something else."

Kids need the gift of your time and your full attention. So does your spouse, or a parent who may be in a home for the elderly.

How do you find the time? First, decide what is more important: Giving time to people who need you or spending time in self-indulgence — bowling, eating out, going to entertainment that pleases only you. Second, schedule your work and other activities more carefully so you have time for people who need your special attention. Say to yourself, "My loved ones are priority one."

GIVE A PERSONAL NOTE. IT'S A POWERFUL GIFT

Recently, I was in the office of a friend who is principal owner of a business grossing over a billion dollars a year. This exceptionally wealthy person could afford to decorate his office walls with costly art. Instead there were framed *handwritten notes* from a prominent golfer, from a senator, and from his minister. These letters, plus two drawings from his grandchildren, were what my friend thought were important to be remembered permanently.

People appreciate receiving a handwritten note. It tells a person, "I am thinking of you and I took time to let you know it."

Personal notes are a wonderful way to tell people you are proud of them for winning a promotion, for becoming an officer in a professional association, for earning an honor, for having a child, or for graduating from school.

A greeting card is fine *if,* and only if, you include a personal message with it. Some people send cards with their name printed. Most of us resent this form of expression. It's too impersonal, too efficient, too automated. It says, in effect, "Our home computer has your name and is programmed to send you this card."

My first impulse on receiving any kind of invitation that doesn't carry a handwritten sentence or two is to throw it away.

Don't use the excuse, "I don't have enough time to write personal notes." In any walk of life, truly important people make time for saying, "Hey, thanks for your help" or "We're eager to see you again." All of our recent Presidents wrote many personal notes per week. Why? Because personal notes are an effective way to win support.

TRY LISTENING. IT'S A POWERFUL GIFT

All people, even the most positive, are, at times, discouraged, disappointed, and hurt. Things may not be going right at work, a teenage child may be in trouble, a marriage or romance may be in jeopardy. When someone you know is down in the dumps, let the person tell you about his or her problem.

Listen, and you give the gifts of understanding, of sympathy, and of support.

Listening does not require you to give advice or solve the person's problem. Resist the temptation to tell the person, "If I were you, I'd do such and such" or "Here's what you should do." Listening means only that you let the other person profit from the therapy of talking out a problem.

The worst punishment that can be inflicted on someone is to deny them the joy of conversation. And the gift of listening, of scrving as a confidante, is more important now than ever before. We are a lonely society. One out of five households is inhabited by only one person. And one half the households consists of only one or two people.

Remember, listening shows love. It tells another person, "I am your friend. I care about you."

Gifts parents and grandparents receive from children are not store-bought; they are pictures the child drew, bird feeders the child made, anything the child created with his or her time and talent. Emerson wrote, "The best gift is part of oneself." When you give part of yourself, you express love, prove to another you care and are sincere.

When you give a possession you prize dearly — maybe a book, a dish, a painting — you are giving a part of yourself. And the gift is certain to be appreciated.

GIVE FAMILY SUPPORT. IT'S GOOD MEDICINE!

Recently, I met John R, an old friend of mine who is a psychologist in a public school system. We both had spent the day attending a seminar on "How to Help Borderline Retarded Young People."

At dinner that evening, I asked John what retarded young people need the most.

John thought for a moment and replied, "There is some medication that may help. I emphasize 'may' because, often as not, the drugs prescribed do more harm than good. The one treatment that does the most good is simply the help of a supportive family or of at least one person who truly wants to help the person with a problem."

"But you're a psychologist," I injected, "I am surprised you didn't say some form of counseling is the best help."

"Not at all," John went on. "Counseling is helpful but *only* if the patient has encouragement — strong, positive encouragement and respect at home. I can help a patient if that person gets positive motivation and respect at home, but not if the individual receives the typical 'put-down' attention most people who need help receive.

"You see," John continued, "I counsel with most of my patients one hour a week. If the person comes from a supportive family, I get good results. I can help the person understand himself better, set goals, modest as they may be, and deal more effectively with other people. But, if the individual's family is not supportive, my service is useless. A negative family can undo in two minutes or less the good I do for the patient in two months."

"Could you be more specific?" I asked John. "Can you cite specific examples that back up your point that the supportive family is the key?"

"OK," John replied. "I'll try. Let me tell you about two young males, J.T. who is seventeen and B.W. who is sixteen, I'm working with now. Both are borderline retardees and both suffer from cerebral palsy and are in wheelchairs. The social-economic backgrounds of both are very similar. But the attitudes of their families about the afflictions of these young men differ greatly.

"In the case of J.T.," my friend continued, "the parents and his brother and sister make J.T. feel like he is unwanted, a burden, and a blight on their lives. He is made to feel guilty because he is holding them back by requiring extra care. In a visit to his home, it was obvious that J.T. 's family didn't like him. J.T. sensed this. Even though the intelligence of a person may be low, a person has a deep sense — an uncanny understanding — of people's attitudes toward him. Even a dog or cat knows whether it is wanted or not."

"It sounds to me like J.T. 's parents may need your services more than he does," I commented.

John smiled and said, "You may be right. But let me tell you about B.W. and his family support system. B.W. is one of the happiest kids I've ever worked with. When I visited B.W. 's home, his mom, his dad, and the two other kids were happy, positive, and progressive. They laughed and enjoyed warm conversation. And B.W. shared in the work detail. He had his chores to do. He did what they called 'floor work' — dusting chairs, cleaning off the dinner table, that sort of thing — because, as his mother joked, 'He is closest to it' (being in a wheelchair and unable to stand).

"Now at school," John went on, "their behavior is very different. J.T. is sullen, is unsmiling, and is hurt by the ridicule that school brats and bullies inflict on someone who is 'different'.

"But B.W. — that's a different story. The stalls in the bathroom won't accommodate a wheelchair. So he simply crawls into a stall when he needs to go to the toilet. He laughs a lot.

"In a few years," John went on, "B.W. will be able to get a job of some kind. He will never be normal, but he will be happy. But not J.T. In his case, I'd say the odds of his ever being able to be gainfully employed are nil."

"You make a strong case for a positive support system to help mentally retarded young people," I commented. "But does this 'medicine' have applications to other psychological problems?" I asked.

"Oh, you bet it does!" John responded. "Take alcoholism. Not one alcoholic in a hundred can get off the drug unless at least one other person provides strong, continuing support. The concept behind Alcoholics Anonymous is tremendous. *If* the alcoholic *truly* wants to break the addiction, and *if* the alcoholic has understanding, supportive people behind him, success can be achieved.

To overcome any kind of obstacle, a person needs the support of another person who really cares. That is a law of psychology. When we in the profession come to realize that, we will have made a giant step forward."

In the past few weeks I've thought a lot about John's parting remark. Each of us *does* need a supportive family or at least a supportive person.

Note this important point: When you give support, you will like and love yourself a whole lot more. And when you need help, seek out a supportive person — someone who doesn't want to judge you, just someone who wants to give you help.

GIVE YOURSELF THE GIFT OF SELF-RESPECT

Here is a rule of successful living. Think about it everyday until you apply it to everything you do.

The rule is: People respect us in direct proportion to how much we respect ourselves. If you think of yourself as a first-class person, others will show you first-class respect. But if your self-concept is "I'm a second-class nobody," you will receive little respect. You are headed straight for the land of nobodies.

No store carries a product called "self-respect," so we cannot buy it. Nor can we inherit self-respect. It doesn't come with the genes. And we can't borrow self-respect from someone who has it.

Self-respect has only one source: One's self.

We don't respect people who sell drugs to children or entice people into prostitution. But each of us has sympathy and spiritual love for the down-and-out winos and derelicts. Somehow, when we see them in their misery, we think to ourselves, "There but for the grace of God go I." But we do not *respect* these unfortunate people because they do not respect themselves.

Meneius, a wise Greek, said 2400 years ago, "A superior person will not show narrow-mindedness or the lack of self-respect." We do not respect the person at work who belittles other people, rides hard over the workers, looks like a bum, and constantly uses profanity. (There are 680,000 words in the American language. Why curse?) The behavior of such people tells us they lack self-respect, so why should we respect them?

Lack of self-respect is instilled in many people by a negative environment. Wives who are physically and mentally abused lose self-respect. Husbands who are put down by their wives and compared unfavorably to other men almost always lose self-respect. And children who are told "Can't you make better grades?", "If I catch you using drugs, I'll beat you within an inch of your life," and "The way you behave embarrasses me," are sure to lose self-respect and acquire behavior patterns that lead to trouble.

So, lack of self-respect is not confined to people in our missions, prisons, and correctional institutions.

HOW JOHN STOOD UP FOR HIMSELF AND WON RESPECT

A challenge facing all people is to display deep self-respect and to gain the admiration and esteem of others. A young manager named J.T. explained how, after being put down to the point his self-respect was in danger, took control and now is highly regarded.

J.T. began, "I got a job as assistant controller of a wholesale distributing company. I know I lacked confidence. I was young, relatively inexperienced and, perhaps most important, I have a speech defect. Well, I guess I felt and looked inferior. Soon I found the president of the company — a real autocrat — was putting me down at our weekly management meeting. Every Monday morning, I was the brunt of one or two jokes. I was always the person picked on to get the chief an ash tray, a glass of water, or perform some other menial task. The chief knew I didn't enjoy this second-class treatment, and knowing this seemed to make him want to belittle me even more.

"His treatment began to get to me. And instead of easing up, the belittling got worse.

"One night before a meeting, I had a long talk with myself. I went over some basics. I reminded myself that I knew my job and I was performing it well. I made up my mind I would not put up with the chief's sarcasm, the sick jokes aimed at me, and the slave treatment any longer.

"At the next meeting, the chief berated me by making a joke about my speech problem. A few minutes later, he made humiliating remarks about a small mistake I had made in a report.

"Immediately after the meeting, I saw the president privately and said to him, 'Sir, for six months now I've endured your humiliating me. Why you do it, I don't know. I assume I am well qualified or you wouldn't have hired me. I assume further I'm doing a good job or you would have fired me. I respect myself too much to put up with being treated like this any longer. So, I quit.' "

"What happened then?" I asked.

"Well," J.T. went on, "I left the room, went to my office and started to pack. In less than five minutes, the chief was in my office, apologizing profusely, and begging me to stay.

"I stayed, and at the next meeting the chief humbled himself and sincerely apologized to the other managers for his conduct. Since then, he has treated me with great respect. The incident happened about nine months ago and I've already received a major promotion."

The point: When you are unfairly treated, speak up politely, but firmly. Tell the put-downer what you don't like about the treatment you receive. Remember, when you respect yourself, others will, too.

STAND UP AND BE COUNTED

A friend in the newspaper business made a comment to me about the widespread lack of self-respect in our society.

"We take pride in referring to our nation as the land of the free and the home of the brave. But a lot of people don't feel free and they don't act brave."

"What do you mean, people don't feel free and act brave?" I asked.

"Everyday we get a huge pile of letters to the editor," my friend continued. "Typically, at least ninety percent of them find fault with politicians, with ideas, with products, with companies, with schools, and with the courts. You name it and people criticize it.

"What bothers me," my newspaper friend went on, "is that only one person in ten who complains about something signs his or her name. Does this sound as if people feel brave? I've concluded, after three decades in this business, that most people are cowards. If someone doesn't respect his viewpoints enough to sign them, we just put them in the trash."

Lack of self-respect explains why many people want to be in that mass called "anonymous."

People who speak out in public (zoning hearings, PTA meetings, or conventions) prove they have self-respect. You may not agree with what they say, but you and others respect them because they speak out.

WHAT TO DO WHEN THAT "I'M-A-NOBODY" FEELING GRABS HOLD

When things go wrong in our work or family life, it is tempting to stop respecting ourselves and to surrender, not to carry on. When a feeling of diminished self-worth sets in, remember these points:

1. *You are unique.* No one else has your fingerprints, your voice, your stature, or, as the bloodhounds demonstrate, your body scent. More important, no one else has your mind. You are different in all ways that count from each of the other five billion human beings on earth. Not one of the hundreds of billions of people who preceded you was like you. And none of the trillions of people who will follow you will be exactly like you.

2. *You are needed.* None of you were put here only to take care of yourself. Other people — a mate, children, employees, neighbors, customers, parents, brothers, and sisters — need you. Your friendship, your love and support, your guidance, and your talents are yours to share.

3. *You are an example-setter.* Each of you is being copied more than you know. Your attitudes, your habits, and your viewpoints are examples other folks try to imitate. Self-respect is an important example to set — to take pride in teaching others.

Keep these points in mind:

- The more you give, the more you'll get. Giving makes you feel wonderful. And it is an investment that pays.
- Think: A dozen is really thirteen. Always give people more than they bargained for.
- Smart people add to — they never take away. Give something extra when you sell something.
- To move ahead, do more than is required. Remember, when

you've mowed the lawn, trim the shrubs.
- A great gift expresses, "I *care* about you!"
  - Give morale-building phone calls.
  - Give the gift of your time.
  - Give a personal note.
  - Listen. It's a powerful gift.
- Give family support. It's good medicine.
- Give yourself the gift of self-respect. Stand up and be counted. Keep in mind people respect us in proportion to how much we respect ourselves.

Chapter 6

Successful Techniques for Motivating People to Do What You Want

Learn this principle of achievement well: We are successful in direct proportion to how well we motivate other people. What we gain in money, influence, and power depends on what we cause other people to do. To succeed in selling, salesmen must persuade other people to buy. To achieve in management, you depend on the support of others to help do the work. To win an election, politicians must get citizens to vote for them. To profit, merchants are dependent on consumers to buy their merchandise. Your success, then, depends on what you cause other people to do — work, buy, invest, sacrifice.

In whatever we do, we must have the support of others. To advance yourself through other people requires winning their cooperation. And the help of others must be voluntary. You can't force people to support you. Nor will you gain much by begging or pleading.

Think for a moment how much your success depends on your motivational skill. You need motivational know-how to get your kids to do homework, to get an appointment with someone difficult to see, to encourage your employees to put forth their best effort, and to induce someone to buy your product, proposition, plan, or idea.

Winning power and influence through skillful motivation can be learned. Let's see how.

SHOW PEOPLE HOW TO PROSPER

There is a lot of advice being passed around on how to enjoy greater prosperity. Much of it is prefaced with "You ought to,"

"You ought to do a better job," "You ought to sell more," "You ought to live a better life," "You ought to make better grades."

The problem is the folks who tell you "you ought to" don't explain how you can make their prescription for you work.

A story illustrates the importance of showing how. An "expert" was asked how to become a millionaire. The "expert" said, "It's simple. All you do is deposit one hundred thousand dollars in a bank each week for ten weeks. Then you'll be a millionaire."

"But where do I get one hundred thousand dollars every week?" the would-be millionaire asked. The expert replied, "That's your problem. I've given you the general strategy. You work out the details."

In getting the best from people, the details become important. The big strategy is not enough. To get great performance from people, you must show them *how* to do what you want them to do.

A friend of mine is amazingly successful in a multi-level marketing business he and his wife started from scratch. Now this fine couple has a net worth of $10 million and an enthusiastic organization of 7,000 people. The business earns the couple $24 per person per month or about $2 million per year.

I asked him to explain why he and his wife were so successful whereas many people tried but didn't make it.

"Well," my friend replied, "our product line is the best. But the secret to success is, first, bringing people into the business and, second, showing them how to succeed — by moving the product and bringing their friends into the business as distributors.

"When we got into the business, we had virtually no help. It was a struggle. We learned how to bring people in and teach them how to succeed by trial and error. A lot of what we tried didn't work. But we kept on experimenting. Our enterprise grew slowly but surely. And we put together two plans to give to the people who joined our business. The first is 'how to recruit people' and the second is 'how to sell products.' "

"But isn't that basic to successful multi-level marketing?" I asked.

"Oh, sure," my friend agreed, "but we don't just tell our prospective associates what to do. We *show* them how to do it. It's easy to tell people they can prosper in our business. It's not hard to build some initial enthusiasm. Everyone, you see, wants more money. But unless we *show* people how to earn more, their enthusiasm soon dies."

"Could you be more specific?" I asked.

"OK. Let me illustrate," my friend went on. "We just don't tell people a product is good. We *show* them. A thirty-second demonstration of a product is worth more than a three-thousand-word written or verbal description. We don't just tell our people to invite folks they know to join the business. We *show* them how — the technique of inviting, of what to say, of when to say it, and of how to get a commitment from them to join us. Details, specifics — they are crucial."

My friend's secret for success boils down to *show how.* And this "help-others-prosper" technique works every time you want another person to do something.

- The minister who tells people to not yield to temptation gets far better results when he shows them, step by step, *how* to resist the urge to try drugs or cheat on an exam.
- It's easy for a parent to tell a child he or she has the ability to make better grades. But it's more rewarding to explain specifically *how* to study and get better scores.
- The coach who shows a player how to catch a pass will see more receptions than if he simply urges him to try harder to catch a pass.

HOW A HELP-THE-CLIENT-MAKE-MONEY BROKER WON A NEW ACCOUNT

An investor told me why he switched stockbrokers. "About two years ago, I opened an account with Brokerage House A," my friend explained. "I don't pretend to be a sophisticated investor, so I put a lot of confidence in my broker. After all, he represented one of the largest firms in the industry, so I assumed he was thoroughly competent. (My friend made an unwise assumption; some of the worst brokers represent prestigious firms. The discount brokerage industry owes its existence to customer dissatisfaction with brokers from old-line firms.)

"Anyway, my investments seemed to be doing OK — not great,

but OK. Then a broker with another firm asked to talk to me about my portfolio. I explained that I was reasonably satisfied with my investments with Brokerage House A, but if he wanted to give me his opinion to go ahead.

"In a few days, the second broker approached me again and asked me questions, such as, 'Why did you buy these bonds?' 'What prompted you to buy these mutual funds?' All I could say was I simply followed the advice of my broker.

"The second broker told me as gently as he could that seven of the ten investments in my portfolio were 'house specials', meaning that the broker received a bonus commission by unloading the securities on me.

"Then the second broker told me something very significant. He said, 'Your broker is more interested in making money *from* you, not *for* you.' In other words, my broker, acting selfishly, was selling me securities that made him the most money, not securities that would likely make me the most money.

"Needless to say, I switched my account to the second broker. It's too early to tell whether I'll make more money with the new broker, but I feel better. I feel like the first broker fooled me and I don't like that."

Note that the first broker thought he was making more money by selling securities that carried a premium commission. But over time, he lost money for himself; he lost what could have been a profitable account.

A rule of success is to ask, "What can I do to help my customers make the most money?" Whether you're in banking, real estate, insurance, securities, or in business for yourself, *put the interests of the customer ahead of your immediate interests and you'll make far more money.* It's the repeat business that makes you the real money.

There is wisdom in the saying "Give a person a fish and he can live a day; teach a man *how* to fish and he can live a lifetime." A peace corps volunteer who shows tribesmen *how* to grow more food is doing them more good than 100,000 leaflets. Show people *how* to get a job and they will get a job. Telling them, "You ought to go to work" or "See so-and-so. They may have something," in no way shows people how to get work. It only exercises the vocal apparatus of the employment agency employee.

The point: *Help people by showing how, not just telling what.*

Showing always works better than telling. Try this example. Take off your jacket and ask a friend to tell you exactly how to put it on. Do exactly what your friend says and, five minutes later, you probably still won't be wearing the jacket and your friend will be totally frustrated!

Or try to tell a child how to tie a shoelace. Unless the telling is supported by some careful showing, the youngster will never learn.

To get results in any activity — selling, making a speech, operating a computer, driving a car, making money, people respond best when you patiently and clearly demonstrate *how*. Give a stranger only verbal instructions about where to find an address and he'll have a hard time finding it. Show by drawing a map where the location is and he'll find it.

Showing is education in its purest and best form.

MASTER THE POWER OF PRAISE TO INFLUENCE PEOPLE

All people crave praise — good nutritional food for their egos. Giving people sincere compliments — demonstrating that they are important and that you recognize them as individuals — is a powerful motivational tool that expands your influence. Praising people helps you get what you want. Here is how.

TELL PEOPLE THEY LOOK GOOD

Everyone wants to hear "You look great!" People buy clothes, have their hair done, lose weight, lift weights, and exercise because they want to feel better about themselves. But they also want the improvement to be noticed. The "profit" that people expect from their investment in looking better is your appreciation of their appearance.

Take notice of efforts other people take to make themselves more attractive. I often buy coffee in a small sandwich shop operated by a fine foreign-born lady in her 70s. One day I noticed the lady had her hairstyle changed. I mentioned how nice I thought it looked. She blushed with appreciation like a girl of 14. I had made her day. From then on, her service was extra-special.

Develop the habit of commenting on how good people look. It costs nothing, yet the rewards to the person you compliment are great. And you'll feel better, too. Do this, and they will take even more pride in their appearance.

I have used a simple psychological test in group situations hundreds of times to identify personal insensitivities. On a scale of one to four, it is unusual to find someone who rates himself or herself four — "I feel I always present a favorable appearance." Most people feel very insecure about how they look. So, put some warmth in other people. Keep in mind that people jog, exercise, visit hair stylists, buy clothes and go on diets hoping to hear "You're looking great!" Know this, too. Tell a person how good they look and they will remember you and what you said for days, maybe weeks.

Why do people buy fur coats? A friend who is a furrier in Houston made a revealing comment to me. "It's not only wealthy women who purchase furs. In fact, Nancy Reagan as First Lady rarely wears a fur coat. Over fifty percent of the furs I sell that are priced over five thousand dollars are bought on lay-away or some other form of credit.

"Now the typical woman in Houston," he continued, "will wear a fur coat about ten times a year. If she keeps the fur five years, it costs her one hundred dollars per wearing."

"One hundred dollars per wearing is a lot of money," I observed. "What motivates people to buy something they don't need?" (It was mid-January and the temperature was 85 in Houston.)

"Two things," the furrier explained. "First, to make other women a little envious, and, second, to make men admire them."

People *do* want to be complimented for looking good. People from 2 to 92 years of age, rich people, poor people, male, female — from parking lot attendants to conservative executives — thirst to feel that people notice them.

SAY SOMETHING GOOD ABOUT A PERSON'S FAMILY

To most of us, our family is our deepest concern. The family is a person's chief interest and biggest source of pride.

Simple comments, such as "How's Jimmy doing in school?" "I'll bet you're proud Sara's involved in ballet." "Jim told me Harriet (the person's wife) is really going places in her job." "Tell Fred (your friend's husband) I am proud he got promoted." "Hey, I heard young Pete is enrolled in the state university. That's great!" Make people know you care about what is important in their lives.

One word of caution: Don't praise another person about his or her family just so you can brag about yours. That only detracts from the joy and satisfaction you want the other person to feel. People don't want to hear why you are great; they want to hear why they are great.

RECOGNIZE OTHER PEOPLE'S ACCOMPLISHMENTS

A key incentive people have for accomplishing something is to receive positive recognition from others. All people want to be complimented for what they do. A salesperson who has worked hard to get a new account deserves and needs recognition for the achievement. An athlete who makes a difficult play successful wants to hear congratulations. A computer programmer who simplifies a system wants to know his work is appreciated.

Accomplishments come in all sizes, from Johnny making an A to Jenny taking her first step and to Grandpa getting elected to the board of directors. But, regardless of whether it is a million dollar achievement or something as simple as a bulldozer operator getting the job done in three hours under schedule, it deserves a pat on the back. And back-patting is excellent motivational medicine. It tells another person, "You are important. Keep up the good work." So, watch what people do that is good and praise them for it. Tell them in person, phone them, or write them a note. They will appreciate it and your influence will grow.

ADMIRE PEOPLE FOR THEIR POSSESSIONS

People buy homes, cars, furniture and other products for two reasons: They need them and they want to receive admiration, and maybe some envy, from other people. So at every opportunity, take note of another person's possessions and express your approval. Say, "I really like your new car. It fits your personality," or "Your apartment is so carefully decorated," or "Your new watch really looks good."

Expressing approval of another person's possessions costs you nothing and proves you admire that person. In return, besides a "thank you," you get better cooperation, harder work, and greater sacrifice.

COMPLIMENT PEOPLE ON THEIR IDEAS

It is unfortunate but true, at work, at home, at school, and at social activities, people are conditioned to think, "My intelligence isn't all that great. People think I'm stupid and naive." That explains why people often fail to give an opinion, don't speak up, and are afraid to try for promotions. As you grow toward greater success, you need all the suggestions, recommendations, and ideas you can get.

The best way to turn on the brain power of others is to praise them at every opportunity. Comments, such as "Joan, I appreciate your judgment — what do you think?" "Bill, I know you've had a lot of experience in similar problems. What do you think we should do?" Or, "George, you did a great job in a similar situation. What do you recommend we do?"

If you use ego-building questions to turn on the intellectual engines of other people, you pay people a strong compliment and you often get useful ideas.

Keep in mind, most people are rarely made to feel, "I have a brain. I have ideas. I have ability." Appeal to the hunger all people have to feel intelligent, and your influence over them expands. It's motivation at its best and costs you nothing.

PRAISE PEOPLE FOR TRYING

In any activity, whether it's making a sales presentation, running a football play, or learning to walk, setbacks are common. Most people who run for a political office lose. Most people who apply for a job are told "No" and most people who enter a contest don't win it.

Effort expended, even if unsuccessful, deserves sincere praise. Not every child can make all A's. The kid who brings home a report card with some C's needs understanding, encouragement, and help — not ridicule, threats, or scolding.

A salesperson in a slump needs praise for making an honest effort. The daughter who doesn't win a beauty contest needs admiration for having entered. The politician who loses an election deserves our commendation for at least trying.

Read these words of President Theodore Roosevelt:

> "It is not the critic who counts; not the man who points out how the strong man stumbled, or where the doer of deeds could have done better. The credit belongs to the man who is actually in the arena; whose face is marred by dust and sweat and blood; who strives valiantly; who errs and comes short again and again; who knows the great enthusiasms, the great devotions, and spends himself in a worthy cause; who at the best knows in the end the triumph of high achievement; and who at the worst, if he fails, at least fails while daring greatly; so that his place shall never be with those cold and timid souls who know neither victory nor defeat."

—Theodore Roosevelt

Remember, how we treat people when they are down affects directly their ability to get up. It is a good habit to congratulate a person when they have tried but failed. It is also smart. People will appreciate and remember your keep-on-trying comments and in one way or another you'll be rewarded. Praising people when they lose is like putting money in the bank.

PASS ON THIRD-PARTY COMPLIMENTS AND WIN A FRIEND

A sure way to win influence with another person is to pass on something positive a third person said about him or her, by making comments, such as "I met Jim W. recently and he told me you're doing great in your new job," "Jill S. asked me to tell you hello the next time I saw you," "Mable G. told me you have a wonderful new home."

The third-party compliment is powerful. It tells the person you're talking to "You are popular. You are respected. You are admired." And when the person you are meeting feels better about himself or herself, doing business is a lot easier. The busy executive hearing some third-party praise now "finds time" to hear what you want to say. The manager who has no job opening will listen to your qualifications and the popular person at a party will remember you later.

And third-party praise is unexpected (surprisingly few people use it). This makes the remark "So and so said something good about you" especially powerful.

All people seek the approval and admiration of others. You become a hero when you give them proof that other people like what they are doing.

Remember, people like to hear good news especially when a third person said it. Make it a rule to have third party good news for everyone you meet.

IF PRAISE IS SO POWERFUL, WHY IS THERE SO LITTLE OF IT?

Chances are, you are criticized far more often than you are praised. It is natural, then, to think criticism is the way to get results. A collection of don't-praise-people myths influences the way we think. Look at them and see how foolish they are.

"But Jim doesn't praise me. Why should I compliment him?" Answer: Because you are a student of success and Jim obviously isn't. Remember, you need Jim's support. As a rule of thumb, plan to give five times as much praise as you receive. Certainly, you want praise, but don't expect it.

"But there is nothing about Sally that is worthy of praise." Answer: There is something about everyone that is praiseworthy. Everyone has some good qualities. Find them and recognize them. No one is perfect and no one is totally imperfect.

"But you can overpraise people." Answer: I have asked thousands of people if they have ever gotten psychological indigestion because they receive too much praise. I haven't found one. Each of us hungers for more ego food.

"But if I praise someone, he or she will put forth less effort." Answer: Wrong! Praise a child for a good report card and the youngster tries even harder. Praise an athlete for a good game and he'll try even harder in the next contest.

TALK ABOUT WHAT IS GOOD AND AVOID GOSSIP

One way to measure a person's success potential is whether they are addicted to gossiping. Gossip is negative conversation. Based on rumor, it is not true information. Gossip is always distorted. And its goal is to make other people worry and become nervous and frustrated. Gossip and leadership do not mix.

We find gossipers at work in all organizations trying to shoot down what positive thinkers are working to accomplish.

Consider this example:

You are seated in the company cafeteria sipping coffee while contemplating a problem about your work.

Harry, the departmental gossip, comes over and says, "May I join you?"

You're polite and say, "Sure."

Harry barely has his coffee and Danish off his tray before he says, "Just heard some important news. There's talk going around that the head honchos are going to cancel Project Three. When that happens, a lot of you guys working on the project will be in deep trouble."

For the next ten minutes you listen to Harry's "evidence" and how this development will impact on job reassignments, layoffs, and terminations.

Now you're back at your desk, worried, confused, and upset. You ask yourself, "Will I be transferred? Maybe fired? If I'm transferred or fired, how will this affect things at home? How will I keep up the payments? Will my wife be willing to give up her job if I am transferred?"

You spend the rest of the day frustrated. You take your concerns home and pass them on to your wife. Now there are two worried people.

Your worries keep on for the next three days. Your productivity slips. Physically, you feel awful.

Then three days later, an official announcement is made that work on Project Three is to be accelerated, not terminated as the gossiper had forecast.

You worried, became sidetracked in your work, and dumped some of your alarm on your wife simply because you let the department's number one gossiper frighten you with manufactured, untrue information.

SOME PEOPLE BELIEVE THE GOSSIPERS

As you program yourself for larger success, keep this fact in mind: Most people are deeply insecure. They run scared at work, in the home, and in social situations. Because people are afraid, they believe the bad news and distrust the good. Let me cite an example.

Brenda Z. was a Ph.D. student in a western university. Brenda was not a standout student and was having trouble passing her program. But she was attractive — and perhaps seductive. She realized that for her to acquire the degree some strong emotional support from her committee of three faculty members would be required.

Brenda recalled a comment the departmental chairman had jokingly once made to her. The chairman had said to her, "You're so attractive, I can't concentrate when I'm around you." Nothing suggestive was meant by the comment. It was intended to be a morale booster.

But Brenda, as with all gossipers, was a schemer. She realized the potential in the chairman's remark. So, timing things perfectly, she approached the youngest faculty member on her committee and, with carefully produced tears, told him the chairman had propositioned her and she would have to drop out of the program. "I won't have sex with him just to get a degree," she said.

The young professor, not suspecting for a moment that the chairman was being framed, did not know what to do. Unfortunately, he took the news, in confidence, of course, to a manipulator of people, the chief gossiper, who happened to detest the chairman.

The head gossiper took over. Quietly he made the rounds of the entire faculty, "Have you heard how the chairman is trying to take advantage of Brenda? I understand the chairman is using his position for sexual advantage."

Soon the dean and other senior administrators knew the whole story — by this time, greatly exaggerated with many fictitious details filled in. Fortunately, the dean investigated it, discovered it was gossip, and reassured the chairman.

And Brenda dropped out of the program.

AVOID THE GOSSIP TRAP

Gossipers are everywhere. It takes skill to avoid the damage they can do. Here are three suggestions:

1. *Don't listen to gossip.* Remember, gossip does you no good. When everybody's "friend," the gossiper, approaches you with a comment, such as "Did you hear about Joan's latest problem?" or "Well, I guess I really started a fracas this morning," or "I heard from a good source that Bill has been padding his expense account," simply say "Joe, I've no time for chit-chat. I'm really pushed right now — got to get a report to the tenth floor before lunch" or something similar, and change the subject, steering Joe's mind in another direction.

It may take time, but once Joe the gossiper knows you are not a negative conversationalist, he'll stop bothering you.

Be too busy to have lunch, coffee, or socialize with people you know enjoy spreading negative news. Search out positive people — the people with constructive plans. You'll enjoy life more.

2. *Remember, your time and talents are the raw materials of your fortune.* Time spent listening to "Here's another dumb mistake the company is making" or "Why did the boss hire that dud?" is subtracting wealth from your account. It destroys time you can use to your advantage and it focuses your talent in a negative direction. Also, if your conscience is in the right place, you know it is wrong to gossip. This makes you feel guilty and displeased with yourself.

A wise professor once told our class, "What you repeat from a conversation will either help you or hurt you. Say bad things about the person you met and something bad will come your way. But, say good things to another about a conversation and you can be sure something good will come your way."

Gossip hurts the gossiper because he or she proves he or she is a small, petty, and negative thinker. Gossip hurts the person being gossiped about for some folks will believe the rumor and repeat it. Gossip hurts the listener because it directs their attention toward negative suggestions.

3. *Assume what you say to another person will be distorted and repeated.* Remember, if you fall into the gossip trap, odds are overwhelming what you say to the gossiper will be distorted and repeated. Probably not one person in 20 will keep confidential information confidential. So, when you say anything to another person about your business plans, your problems, your goals, or your views, don't be surprised if other people soon hear a version of what you told a "friend" in confidence.

Unless you *know* the person you are talking with is a true confidant, you must assume what you say to that person will be repeated and with negative embellishment. Tell A that Tom is overweight and A will likely tell B that you said Tom is too fat to walk. Tell Jane that Barbara is unsatisfactory and Jane will likely tell Sandra that Barbara really "goofs things up."

You see, bad news travels fast and gets worse with each telling.

And when you preface what you say by telling another person, "This is highly confidential" or "Please keep this absolutely quiet," you simply whet the desire of the other person to spread the news! The more you encourage others to keep information to themselves, the more they are encouraged to tell others.

Think selfishly for a moment. To achieve your goals of prosperity, peace of mind, recognition, and admiration, you must have the support of other people. Your success is fashioned by what you can cause other people to do for you. You want their support. But even more important, you must have their support. Talk about people, yes. Talk about the bad in people, no.

RESOLVE TO GET AHEAD, NOT GET EVEN

Fair play. We all crave it. Most of us try to treat other people the way we would like to be treated. People *do* want to live by the Golden Rule. But when another person violates the fair play code, we get angry. We want revenge. Even before a child can walk, he or she wants to get even with a sibling who treats him or her unfairly. Bed-wetting may be caused by a child seeking revenge against a parent the young person believes is unfair.

A high school principal wants to teach students a lesson (get even) for annoyingly mischievous conduct by imposing some strict but uncalled-for rules. What happens? The offending kids are joined by model students. Soon lockers are broken into, school property is damaged, morale suffers, and absenteeism increases. Again, everyone loses when those in authority seek revenge.

In every big city, there are "get even" murders everyday. An estranged husband wants to settle the score with his spouse; he takes a gun or a knife — and another life is snuffed out. No one wins in a no-win contest.

The I'm-going-to-get-even-if-it's-the-last-thing-I-ever-do resolution often is just that. Cause of fatal auto accidents may be listed as "reckless driving" or "lost control of the vehicle." The real cause often is an innocent driver, having been nearly run off the road by another motorist, speeds up to "teach" the offending driver a "lesson," and a crash is the result. Who won? No one.

Two summers ago, a baseball star was nearly hit by a pitched ball. The star thought it was deliberate and immediately ran to the mound swinging at the pitcher. In seconds, both teams were engaged in a brawl. Some might say the hitter did what was "right" and that baseball fans want to see an occasional fight. What the batter did not realize was that his "getting even" cost him a product endorsement contract worth a half million dollars! The sponsor decided the player's wholesome image had been damaged.

When terrorists from one nation kill ten innocent people in another nation, counter terrorists in the offended society retaliate and kill 20 people from the terrorists' country. The logic in this situation is that, in time, everyone will be dead.

Revengitis, the get-even disease, is inborn in each of us. "An eye for an eye, a tooth for a tooth" at face value seems like an intelligent way to deal with those who take unfair advantage. But getting even drains our energy, is always short-sighted, and takes our mind off the big objective. Success and revengitis don't mix. We can deal positively with the desire to get even. But it takes work. Study these examples to see how to get ahead instead of get even.

HOW TO DEAL WITH "I-WANT-TO-GET-EVEN" SITUATIONS

Getting even at best leads to mediocrity. Revenge is not a success habit. Look at these ways to handle common "I-want-to-get-revenge" situations.

Revenge-Tempting Situation	The Easy but Wrong Way to Deal with Get-Even Desire	The Difficult but Right Way to Handle Revenge Situations
Mature woman has sister who ignores her achievements, puts her down as she does other family members.	Counter attack by ignoring what sister does. "Forget" birthday, refuse to invite her to social gatherings.	Overlook sister's coolness. Find ways to praise her. Be as cordial as possible in the relationship.
Person loves mate but finds she (he) is interested in someone else.	Make accusations, get angry, retaliate with similar behavior. Terminate the relationship.	Find out what the problem is, then correct it. Show more love, affection, forgiveness.
Supervisor gives you an undeserved bad job evaluation.	Spread rumors about the boss. Find way to make his (her) performance look bad. Go to his superior and complain.	Politely ask superior for a reevaluation. Ask advice on how to improve.
Student receives what she (he) feels is an unfair grade.	Go to instructor's superior and complain. Create some unflattering gossip about instructor.	Ask instructor for a reevaluation. Request advice. Ask to retake examination.
Neighbor's dog consistently messes up your yard.	Have your kids drape neighbor's trees with toilet tissue. Call the dog pound. Try to poison neighbor's dog.	Call the problem to your neighbor's attention. Show understanding but seek cooperation.
Another motorist almost hits you at an intersection.	Speed up. Blow your horn. Try to catch person at next intersection, then swear at him. Risk having accident if necessary.	Keep calm. Avoid going to war in an automobile. Pray that the wild driver doesn't hit someone else.
Person at business conference belittles your idea or suggestion. Deflates your ego.	Fight back with a nasty comment. Put the person down. Write a nasty comment and pass it on to your "friends" at the conference.	Avoid arguing. Sincerely show you understand the critic's view. Then elaborate on your ideas.
Results:	You think you're winning but you're really losing. You lose respect, appreciation, help, love, self-esteem.	You may think you're losing but you're really winning. You win cooperation, self-respect, admiration, and the goals you seek.

Remember:

- Everyone wants to prosper. Show people how to earn more and you'll have their support. Ask yourself, "How can I help people enjoy more?" Then *show* them.
- Master the wonderful power of praise.
  - Tell people they look good.
  - Say nice things about their family.
  - Recognize people's accomplishments.
  - Admire their possessions.
  - Compliment people for their ideas.
  - Commend people for trying even if they fail.
- Be sure to pass on third-party compliments.
- Gossip and leadership don't mix. Don't listen to gossip. Keep in mind that what you tell people will be distorted and retold.
- Decide to get ahead, not get even. Conquer revengitis by doing what is right.

Chapter 7

Enthusiasm Plus Action
Equals Success

Think of a brand new extra-special automobile. It's expensive — $50,000. Classic design. First rate. World-class engineering. Beautiful hand-tooled upholstery. A hand-tooled engine.

But there is a problem. The car won't start. Why? Because no one installed an ignition system. In an emergency such as rushing someone to a hospital, that $50,000 car is no more than a pile of junk.

Now think of someone you know who has had all the advantages. By adulthood the person is expensive. At least $250,000 has been spent to feed, clothe, educate, and entertain the individual to prepare for a career. The person's design is great — excellent genes, handsome looks, good health. The engineering is first class — the best schools and college, and the person is well-upholstered in the best clothing.

But, like the car, there is a problem. Johnny simply won't run. He can't get turned on because his psychological ignition system is missing. In the real competitive world, the $250,000 preparation for success is wasted.

Machines and human beings have something in common: They must be turned on to work.

Human beings are born with a psychological ignition system. It's called enthusiasm.

Enthusiasm is completely intangible and invisible. Yet you see its results every day. When you see an athlete break a record, you're looking at enthusiasm in action. A family without much money seeing to it that their kids get a good education, the salesperson who is top producer, the job applicant who gets the job, the "ordinary" person who becomes a millionaire, the individual who changes the way people think, the couple who makes their marriage work wonderfully — these are people with enthusiasm.

Enthusiasm, you see, is psychological adrenalin that makes your mind, body, and will work to ensure victory despite hardship, competition, limited money, and other drawbacks.

Everyone is born with enthusiasm. The first thing a newborn child does is scream with enormous enthusiasm. If an adult yelled, pound for pound, with the same intensity as a newborn, the sound would be heard for a mile!

But soon that honest, wholehearted spirit gets stifled. People begin to monkey with the young person's psychological ignition system. The child hears "don't," "stop that," "you shouldn't," "you ought to know better," "you're dumb," "can't you do anything right?" and other instructions that teach the child to suppress enthusiasm.

Words of commendation, encouragement, and praise are rare. Over a time, the young person finds security by not projecting his or her real personality. Inborn enthusiasm is replaced with conformity. And since conformity is only average, unenthusiastic, and ordinary, by adulthood most people have lost their eagerness for an exciting, positive, joy-filled life.

Attempts have been made to explain what accounts for "genius." Why are some people unusually successful in science, business, the arts, technology?

One theory, popular for years, held that outstanding individuals have bigger brains than "ordinary" people. But experiments in which the brains of "great" people were actually weighed showed no difference from the rank and file of us.

Education is often cited to explain the difference. Yet, Einstein who revolutionized the way we think about physics and Von Braun who pioneered space exploration did not earn Ph.D. degrees. Many of our most successful artists, business executives, entrepreneurs, farmers, and philosophers have limited formal educations. There is, in fact, a real problem with formal education. It lulls people into thinking that because they have a piece of paper, they are assured of success.

A recent Nobel prize winner in chemistry said, "I am completely *obsessed* with chemistry. It is my life. I live to unravel the nature of matter." Obsession or enthusiasm explains his success.

The amount of enthusiasm potential in each of us is unlimited. Each of us is free to use as much enthusiasm as we choose. Use little power and we receive little result. Turn on a lot of power and we receive big success. People achieve what they want in direct proportion to how much enthusiasm they have for what they do. Great success always is accompanied by great enthusiasm. On the other hand, failures are always lacking in enthusiasm.

This chapter shows techniques for making your psychological ignition system work better for you.

SMILE AND YOU MANUFACTURE ENTHUSIASM

Smiling is an amazing motivational tool. Smiling is positive; a frown is negative. Do this little test. Think of someone you don't particularly like. Now, smile as you think about that person and your dislike vanishes. As long as you are smiling, you can't feel anger toward another person.

Or try to worry about a problem at work and smile at the same time. You can't. Smiling wipes away negative feelings like a towel wipes away water. Smiling is a wonderful way to beat success enemies such as disappointment, anger, frustration, disgust, and fear.

Use smiles in all contacts with others. When you meet someone for the first or 100th time, greet the person with a smile. When you're making a statement about a product, a person, or an idea, smile. If someone scolds you, smile and you melt down the other person fast. And when you feel like giving up, make yourself smile.

HUMOR IS POWER. USE IT

When you project humor(sometimes by telling brief anecdotes or quick jokes) or when you see something funny even in difficult situations, other people appreciate, admire, and come closer to you. Humor is like a magnet in drawing people to you. People always like to be around someone who helps them smile, laugh, and enjoy a moment. And people always want to avoid the fault-finder who can't smile and sees only the negative in every situation.

You see, humor works miracles. It literally makes other people feel better physically. Humor reduces blood pressure, promotes relaxation, aids digestion, and helps people forget their worries. For generations, *Readers Digest* has said laughter is the best medicine. It really is.

There's no doubt about it — the people you want to influence see humor as an asset. A young man I know well is about to finish medical school. He is a promising young doctor and applied at 20 leading hospitals to do his residency. He received 19 acceptances. A 95 percent acceptance rate speaks enormously well for this man. Now here is a significant point: Seven of the medical school deans who offered him a residency mentioned the young doctor's sense of humor as being a factor in their decision to accept him.

Here is part of what the chairperson of one hospital wrote to him:

> "Dear Dr. Olt:
> You are able to see the lighter, brighter side when faced with a difficult situation. Your sense of humor will serve you well in your career as a physician."

An exceptional salesman made this comment to me: "In the first few seconds of every presentation, I make it a point to have my prospect smile or, better yet, laugh. I do this for two reasons: First, laughter relaxes and makes the prospect much more receptive to what I want to tell him. Second, laughter helps me build my reputation as a warm friendly person — someone he'll want to talk with next time I call."

The key to humorous self-expression is finding the something amusing in any situation.

Life is too short to spend it being long-faced.

What is the raw material of good humor? The best humorous material is yourself. President Reagan has the ability to find something humorous about himself to fit any occasion — and score points, too. The President makes dozens of funnies about his age. And since he is, by far, the oldest president in history, Mr. Reagan's laughing at himself for being so old disarms those who want to say he is too old for the job.

GET KNOWLEDGE TO GENERATE ENTHUSIASM

An old truism tells us the more we know about something the more we know we don't know. Each new discovery in medicine or engineering or physics raises more questions than it answers. Knowledge also increases enthusiasm.

The more we explore space, the deeper our cameras see, and the more we discover about the structure of matter, the greater is our enthusiasm to learn still more.

A friend who heads an agency to prevent child abuse told me it's difficult for her to raise money, get volunteers, and convince the media to publicize the problem until people understand how widespread mistreatment of children is. Once people know, they are eager to support her work.

Again, enthusiasm comes with knowledge.

Most people are bored with the idea of collecting stamps until they know answers to questions such as who decides what image appears on a stamp and why, how many stamps are issued each year, what makes some stamps exceptionally valuable, who invented stamps, and why all stamps are not the same size.

Knowledge does supply motivation and enthusiasm to learn more.

We take an important step toward developing enthusiasm when learning more about a person, a thing, or an idea. Ignorance inhibits enthusiasm; knowledge expands it.

HELP OTHERS FEEL ENTHUSIASM
AND YOU'LL BE EVEN MORE ENTHUSIASTIC

The adage "The more you give, the more you'll get" applies to enthusiasm. The more encouragement you give other people, the more encouragement you will receive. And the more encouragement you receive, the better job you will do.

Master this concept. Regardless of what you do, your ability to inspire others to give the best they can to achieve a goal is vital to effective leadership. A law of success is this: People who can inspire others become great leaders. People who cannot inspire others never become leaders.

Draw on your experience and, chances are, you can recall one teacher who really got you excited. You studied hard, attended all classes, cooperated, and, above all, learned something of value. And you probably can recall another teacher who turned you off. You studied only to pass the course, cut classes when you could, and learned only enough to pass the course.

What made the difference? Did the inspiring teacher have a degree from a "better" university? Was he or she more intelligent? More experienced? Probably not. The difference was the ability to make students feel enthusiastic.

You see big differences in the quantity and quality of work performed for different superiors, office managers, executives, and supervisors. People who inspire others meet the first requirement of leadership. They know how to encourage, to move, and to guide people toward a goal.

It follows then that answering the question "How can I inspire others?" is important to help you gain money, status, and other rewards of leadership.

When you inspire your people by encouraging them to help in the planning, they perform better. And the better your people do their jobs, the better you look. A leadership maxim says, "You are not judged by what you do; you are evaluated by what you cause your support people to do."

Put the maxim to work, and you'll enjoy more satisfaction, too.

HELP PEOPLE IDENTIFY WITH THE RESULT

Make no mistake: The more closely a person can identify with the end result of his work, the more enthusiastic and productive the individual will be.

A friend who owns a large furniture factory in North Carolina takes enormous pride in his people. And they are mighty proud of him, too. He is a master in helping his personnel identify with what his company does. It is a powerful enthusiasm builder.

"Take my truck drivers," he explained. "They work very hard, never complain, and take more than their share of risks. Our drivers identify with their work. When they deliver a load — maybe two thousand miles away — they sign all documents, 'delivered with pride by _____.' Signing their names makes them think,

'I did it. I delivered this load with my skill, caution, and hard work.' When they phone the office to let us know they've made it, they always begin with, 'This is _____. Mission accomplished!'

"But employee identification doesn't stop there," my friend continued. "A team of three to five employees finish off and inspect each piece of furniture. And their names appear on a neat label. This gives them pride and it sure helps sell the furniture when customers know human beings — not machines — put it together."

Even secretaries in my friend's plant are identified with the letters, reports, price quotations (everything that is typed) not by initial (no one knows peoples' initials) but by name.

Identification with work done is focusing on the big, the important, and it is enthusiasm in action.

BUILD A TEAM THAT PUTS ENTHUSIASM FIRST

It makes no difference what you do, you need the capable and enthusiastic support of other people to reach your goals. To operate your own business, to move ahead in corporate life, to build an athletic team, or to win in politics, requires people to help you. In choosing these people, two qualities are important: ability and attitude.

Ability is important. To develop a great organization requires able people; to have a fine baseball team means talented athletes must be recruited; and to design great buildings needs the contributions of able architects. To achieve any great result requires trained, skilled, and able people.

We live in a period when work is becoming increasingly specialized and complex. The number of job specialties has doubled in the past 15 years and may triple in the next 15. And the percent of our population with a college degree is setting a record. Yet, increases in productivity are disappointing. Why? The reason is that ability only measures what people *can* do; ability does not tell us what people *will* do. There is no multiple choice test that can measure desire or motivation.

Attitude is more important than ability! A person who rates 10 on a scale of 1-to-10 in ability but rates only 5 or 6 in terms of attitude will be outdistanced by a person who rates 5 or 6 in ability but scores 10 in attitude.

With an attitude score of 10, a person can greatly upgrade ability through learning, experience, and effort. The opposite is not true. In every business or profession — in all kinds of jobs — there are people with great ability who perform poorly, drift, "retire" on the job, won't cooperate, and do nothing to advance themselves or the enterprise.

College coaches do a careful job of recruiting outstanding high school players. Scouts tell them what players to observe. Scouts want the best players in action. But every season there are "walkons" — high school players who weren't even considered by the scouts or recommended by the high school coaches — who try out for the college team and make it. Attitude expressed as a burning enthusiastic desire to make the team explains why.

Invariably, people who made it to the top, who truly rate, are at the top of the attitude scale. Ability is important but never as essential as a positive, committed attitude. Ability is only potential power. It has no value until it is turned on.

Positive people will continue to improve; negative people at best will only hold their own.

TO INSPIRE, SHOW PERSONAL INTEREST IN YOUR PEOPLE

I've addressed many awards banquets. Some companies hold an awards function once a year. And that's great. Unusual performance should be recognized because it encourages everyone to do a better job. Everyone needs a pat on the back. People need and appreciate hearing "good job," "thanks," "we appreciate your help," and "keep up the wonderful work."

What is needed to supplement the annual awards function is a day-by-day, week-by-week effort to fuel enthusiasm. And a person won't remain highly enthusiastic about selling, teaching school, playing football, or doing anything else unless he experiences frequent infusions of inspiration.

A sales manager of a software company told me about his motivational program. "I have thirteen representatives east of the

Mississippi," he explained. "My people call only on hospitals and medical facilities. The salespeople are on their own most of the time and they travel a great deal.

"But I talk with each of them at least twice a week. I don't get into the technical side of selling very much. Our people know how to sell. We have an excellent training program. The purpose of my calls is what I call 'slump prevention.' In subtle ways I remind them of their potential and let each of them know I appreciate the job they are doing.

"Believe me," my friend went on, "it takes a world of enthusiasm to keep up one's spirits when you're away from your wife and kids and comforts of home three or four nights a week."

"Do your calls work?" I asked.

"They sure do. You see, attitude and attitude alone is the only way I know to stimulate sales and prevent slumps. I can't control competition. I can't control the budgets of the medical centers we sell. But I do have a big influence over the enthusiasm of my people. And I work very hard to give that enthusiasm a boost."

EVERYONE CRAVES POSITIVE ATTENTION

People resent being treated as machines or lifeless objects. People have wives, husbands, kids, hobbies, pets, problems. Taking a few minutes to let a person talk to you about private affairs is a compliment. One very successful supervisor I know chats two or three minutes a day with each of his 15 people. He told me, "It takes only thirty to forty-five minutes a day and it pays. It helps me keep their respect because I show interest in them."

My friend went on, "Knowing the personal interests and concerns of my people is the most important part of my job."

"A lot of managers I know would say the personal concerns of your people are none of your business," I injected.

"I know that," the supervisor continued. "But let me give you some proof my method works. The year before I was made supervisor, absenteeism because of sickness averaged thirteen days per employee. Absenteeism was only two days per person during my first full year. Productivity is up, turnover is down, and the accident record for my department is perfect.

"It's good business for me to become emotionally involved with my people. After all, their problems are my problems because what bothers them affects me, too."

ENTHUSIASM WORKS MIRACLES

Enthusiasm is the power that spells the difference in selling, sports, and business. Enthusiasm makes people feel and act like winners, so they win.

ENTHUSIASM SELLS HOUSES

Eighty percent of the money earned in selling real estate is made by 20 percent or less of the agents. Why? Is the one agent in five who makes as much as the other four combined more skilled? A harder worker? Have more years in the business? Luckier? No.

The stars in real estate have that spiritual ingredient — enthusiasm. They put life, dreams, pleasure, and opportunity into what otherwise is a dead product. Successful real estate people don't just show a property — they "enthuse" it.

A woman executive, Marianne O., explained to me why she bought a house the second time it was shown her — by a different agent.

"I had been looking for a house since my husband and I were transferred here," Marianne explained. "The agent knew all the facts about each property — square footage, mortgage details, taxes, utility expenses, those sorts of things. She had a factual answer for every question I asked. But after looking at eighteen houses, I still didn't find the right house for us. So, I decided to use another real estate firm.

"The agent from the second firm began by asking me dozens of questions. She said to me, 'Before I show you any house, I want you to tell me what your ideal house would be — what you want it to do for you, your family, and your social life.'

"Well, I told the second agent in some detail what I hoped to find. The agent looked through her files, punched some information into her computer and said to me, 'We have a house that looks perfect for your needs. Let's go see it.'

"When we got to the property I immediately recognized it as one the first agent had shown me and I had turned down. So I said to the agent 'I've seen this house and it just won't do.'

"My new agent replied, 'The owner cancelled his listing agreement with another firm just a week ago. I believe there may be some features about this property that weren't explained to you. Let me show it to you again!'

"A little reluctantly, I agreed. The second agent had the same hard facts as the first. But the second agent made the facts come to life, she reworded them, she was enthusiastic about every feature of the house, of the lot, and of the neighborhood."

"Would you explain?" I asked.

"Well, for one thing, both agents told me the house was energy efficient. But the second agent told me we could expect to save one hundred dollars a month on heating and cooling. And then she said to me, 'One hundred dollars a month is not a large sum these days, but one hundred dollars a month invested over the twenty-year mortgage term paid at fifteen percent would be a nice fortune.'

"The second agent captured my imagination about the lot, too. She had ideas about where to plant trees and showed me a place that would be just right for an old-fashioned small garden.

"Two rooms in the house needed considerable work but the agent explained that was one reason the property was such a value and, besides, I could redecorate them the way I wanted.

"When I asked about the neighbors, she didn't just tell me they are fine upstanding people. She showed me a profile of every one of the eight closest neighbors — ages, occupations, number of children and so forth.

"When the second agent described the high school, (we have two teenagers) she didn't say, 'It's one of the best in the city' — all real estate agents tell you that. She told me about several alumni of the school who are now extremely successful, about some of the awards that students in the band, on the debating teams, and in athletics had received.

"Then she said to me with deep feeling in her voice, 'Thanks for letting me show this property to you. I plain love the potential this home has.' "

"What happened then?" I asked.

Marianne replied, "Twenty-four hours later we owned the home."

The point: Facts alone don't sell anything. Facts projected with enthusiastic imagination is what causes prospects to say "Yes!"

ENTHUSIASM WINS GAMES

Athletic teams once differed greatly in ability, skill, size, and experience. But no more. Baseball teams now typically vary less than one inch in average height, only three or four pounds in average weight, and a month or two in experience. The same is true for football, basketball, hockey, or any other sport.

The difference between competing teams today is not physical; it is spiritual. The team with the deepest desire to win and with the greatest enthusiasm comes out on top!

A football coach told me about his half-time talk with his team which was down 28-0.

"I didn't hash any plays, scold players who had made mistakes, or threaten anyone. I simply told them if the other team could outscore us by twenty-eight points in the first half, we could outscore them by more than twenty-eight points in the second half. I let my team know how great they really were and to play that way. Well, we won the game thirty-three to twenty-eight."

"And that was on the other team's field," I injected.

"It was. But that doesn't make the victory any sweeter to me," replied the coach. "I've conditioned my players to look inward for spiritual strength and not depend on a home field advantage."

The coach made an important point: Enthusiasm makes the difference and enthusiasm comes from within the individual, not from some outside source.

WHY IS ONE RETAILER OUTSTANDINGLY SUCCESSFUL?

The chairman of the leading retailer in Washington, D.C. explained the success of his chain to me.

"We don't have much, if any, advantage over our competitors in the conventional sense. We have good locations and they have good locations. We carry many of the same brands. Three hundred dollars spent in their stores will give the consumer about the same quantity and quality of merchandise as three hundred dollars spent in our stores. We have special sales and they have special sales. We advertise heavily and our competitors do too.

"The critical profit-making advantage we have is our people. Our competitive edge boils down to how the customer is treated. We want people in our stores who put service first, happily and enthusiastically. We will not tolerate employees who act like they are doing a customer a big favor by serving them. We have a policy 'put the customer's complete satisfaction first', and it's followed in every department, in self-service and personal service areas, in dining rooms, and in leased departments throughout the store."

"You must make a major effort to motivate your people to project enthusiasm," I commented.

"Oh, we do," my friend replied. "We have an on-going reward system for superior service. We have motivational meetings — a lot of programs aimed at keeping our people in high spirits.

"But our motivational program really begins in the personnel selection process. We don't simply hire people to fill jobs. We *select* people to act as store representatives. Our image is on the line with each person we employ."

I found that observation to be interesting and I asked my friend to explain.

"Well," he continued, "our personnel people go beyond the usual criteria for employment such as good health, a satisfactory employment history, no criminal record, and good appearance.

"We look for attitudinal factors. We find out in the interviewing process whether the applicant only wants a job or wants a job with us. We don't believe in corporate welfare."

"What do you mean by that?" I asked.

"There are two kinds of welfare," my friend went on. "Most people think only of public or government welfare. But there's another kind I call private or corporate welfare. And if all the statistics were in, corporate welfare — paying people for doing nothing or next-to-nothing — costs our economy more than public welfare. And it sure costs a business a fat sum.

"Corporate welfare is paying people to go through the motions of doing a job but not really to do the job. We try very hard not to put people on our payroll who will give less than a one hundred percent effort.

"We evaluate our applicants in terms of their desire to work with us, to be team players, and to talk, to smile, to act, and to walk like people who are alive and enthusiastic.

"Our personnel people administer what I privately call a 'spirit' test. Through conversation they seek answers to questions, such as 'Does the person have deep pride in himself or herself?' 'Does the applicant understand that pay and performance should be related?' 'Does the person speak well of previous employers?' 'Is the person a self-starter?' 'Will the applicant be a team player?'

My friend added, "Customers don't like to do business with "dead" people. I regard shopping as America's number one form of recreation. If people don't enjoy shopping with us, they'll try to find another store where exchanging their money for merchandise is a happier experience."

In Atlanta there are many airline options for flights to most cities. But my travel agent always books me on one airline, even if it means an hour or two delay. Why? The airline in second place flies the same kinds of equipment, travels to most of the same cities as my preferred airline, and meets the same safety standards. Why then do I insist on flying one airline and not the other?

In two words — *employee enthusiasm.* Personnel on my preferred airline are more enthusiastic than those on others, from the check-in counter to the gate and aboard the aircraft. Seemingly little things like smiles, warm greetings, great service, and friendly good-byes from the pilots made the difference.

Enthusiastic professionalism makes Delta the airline of choice to millions of people. And what does enthusiasm cost Delta? Not a dime. It *makes* money for the company. Any business can earn a big competitive advantage without spending money. People don't just buy products. They want products plus enthusiasm.

BELIEVE IN WHAT YOU DO AND ENTHUSIASM FOLLOWS

When we believe deeply what we do is right, enthusiasm or spiritual involvement follows automatically. Outstanding ministers, statesmen, physicians, and business people who believe what they do is critically important and must be done, always project enthusiasm.

Meanwhile, when we know something is wrong, we cannot put our heart into it. Most of us could never become enthusiastic about selling drugs because our conscience tells us damaging the bodies and corrupting the minds of other people is wrong.

Your conscience never lies to your body. How we honestly feel toward a person, object, or idea shows in our eyes, handshake, voice, and mannerisms.

A successful actor explained to me why he is offered more roles than he can accept and earns a large income when most actors are out of work.

"Most actors act like actors," he began. "The typical actor pretends, feigns, fakes the role he or she plays. They don't bury themselves in the role. I concentrate so deeply on being the person I play that I become that person. The best acting is not pretending to be a person — it is *being* that person. When I let the personality of the role I play become my personality — my mannerisms, behavior, voice, timing — my whole being is the role.

"Now," he went on, "if, in reviewing a part, I think I cannot become the personality of the role, I reject it. People know if you are faking. A phoney always comes across as just that — a phoney. To be a great actor, you must have credibility; you must believe you are the role you play."

A salesman told me, "I flatly refuse to sell a product I don't believe is right for customers. If I don't think it's good for their purposes, they invariably will sense how I feel and my credibility will be damaged. I represent only products I can be enthusiastic about."

A trial lawyer said, "When I am convinced a client is innocent, I simply do a better job in the courtroom than if I feel the person may be guilty. Juries always know whether I believe what I say in a client's defense."

The point: To win the support of people, you must believe in what you say and do. Enthusiasm is a by-product of belief. Successful people know it makes sense to let their conscience guide them.

PUT ENTHUSIASM IN WHAT YOU SAY

When talking, the words you speak are important. But your sound is even more important than your words. You can say, "Good morning, you look great today" so the sound the person hears ranges from "That person really cares about me and thinks I'm terrific" to "That person doesn't mean what he says — he really thinks I look awful."

Experiment with a few phrases and see how many distinctly different emotions you can project. Phrases like, "How are you?" "I'm glad to meet you," and "I like your new car" can be said to express friendliness, sarcasm, envy, or joy.

All human emotions are expressed in sound. People who study music know there are sounds to express love, excitement, tenderness, sadness, and the many other feelings music writers want to project.

If you have a dog or a cat, you know how the pet feels by the sounds it makes. And months before a child says its first word, the infant expresses clearly how he feels about you, about food, and about objects in his environment.

When you meet someone who doesn't speak your language, you still recognize the emotions that person conveys to you. Sound, not words, is the basic message.

Sound is also largely neglected in communication. Kids are taught how to say words correctly; they are not taught to speak them enthusiastically.

Put these two enthusiasm-building tools to work when you speak:

Remember, to win a friend, be a friend. So tell yourself I *like* this person and your voice tone automatically projects the warmth you want to convey.

Speak with spirit. Sound strong, vigorous. No one likes to talk to "dead" people. Put lots of life in your voice.

HOW TO PROJECT ENTHUSIASM ON THE TELEPHONE

Next to face-to-face conversation, the telephone is our most important vehicle for talking to people.

Electronic telephone technology has taken huge leaps forward in recent decades. But human technology in using the phone positively has not.

A friend jokingly told me that if we drove our cars as badly as we use the telephone, no one would be alive!

Picture-phone technology has been around for 25 years. Yet the miracle of being able to talk to someone across town or across the world by telephone and see them while you speak is immediately translated into pictures in our mind without the aid of technology. People do, in a sense, "see" another person over the phone. A person calling us "sees" us emotionally just as clearly as if that person were sitting across a table from us.

1. When you answer the phone, follow this easy, business-like, four-step method:

- Greet the person warmly with "Good morning," "Good afternoon," or "Good evening."
- Identify your business or organization — "James Wilson Company."
- Identify yourself, "Ted Brown speaking."
- Offer assistance, "How can I help you?"

At most, this takes five seconds or eight percent of a minute.

2. *Smile while you talk.* A smile gives you confidence and projects "I am positive." When you smile on the phone, you are in control of the communication. When you put a genuine smile — a real I-am-glad-to-be-talking-to-you expression on your face — you cannot be angry, afraid, or express any negative emotion. And the person you are talking to will be receptive to what you are saying. When you sound positive and confident, the person you're talking with feels in good hands.

3. *Speak slowly on the phone.* Talk at the same rate you would talk if the person were seated across from you. Normal talk speed is far more efficient. Just as fast drivers on crowded expressways cause accidents that cause bumper-to-bumper slowdowns, fast talking over the phone wastes time by making it necessary to repeat the message ("I'm sorry, I didn't understand" or "Would you please repeat. We must have a bad connection.") Fast talking also results in being connected with the wrong person or department.

I return many telephone calls and I estimate that in 50 percent of my returns, the receptionist answers the phone so badly I cannot recognize the name of the company I'm calling. The receptionist blurts out the name of the company so fast, it sounds like an audio tape speeded up three times.

Note this: Fast speaking on the phone indicates insecurity and lack of confidence. Slow speech — the normal conversational rate — suggests, "I'm confident." "I'm in control."

"But, how do I handle mean people who call?" Many calls come from complainers: "There must be a mistake in the bill you sent," "You sent me something I didn't order," "Jimmy came home from school all upset and it's so and so's fault," and "You didn't pick up my garbage."

Two observations: First, there are no really "mean" people. The person who calls to complain is a member of the human tribe — one of your kinfolk.

Second, the complainer is not angry with you. He is mad at himself. You are simply the fall guy, the scapegoat. Think of yourself as a therapist helping someone by receiving the brunt of his anger.

Don't take complaints personally.

Note to executives: *Monitor the calls your business receives.* An airline I know well monitors one percent of all calls received by reservation people. The purpose is not to spy but to bring about corrective action in its training program. Smart managers of hotels, of car rental companies, of department stores, of governmental agencies, and of other big users of the telephone can profit enormously from taping a sample of calls to make sure people receive courteous, efficient service.

(If you have a business, have a friend call your office and see what kind of reception he or she receives. Then take corrective action as needed.)

No company wanting to make money permits its outside sales representatives to dress like slobs, smell like garbage, and insult customers. Yet many, many businesses have people answering the phone who speak like slobs, sound like garbage, and deserve a prize for insulting and intimidating people who call the business.

All people who use the telephone are part of the sales team. Everyone using the phone from the night watchman to the company president projects an image of the business.

Every business exists to *sell something*. And selling that something is a lot easier when the image projected over the phone is "We like you. We're glad you called. We want to help you."

To make enthusiasm work miracles for you, remember:

- *Enthusiasm is your psychological ignition system.* People succeed in direct proportion to their ability to turn on their enthusiasm.
- *Enthusiasm works "miracles"* in selling, in business, in sports, and in rearing a family. Success and enthusiasm go together.
- *Believe in what you do and enthusiasm follows.* If you don't believe something is right, don't do it.
- *Put enthusiasm in what you say.* Your sound is more important than the words you speak. Put spirit in your voice. Let your voice say, "I *am* glad to talk to you."
- *Smile and you manufacture enthusiasm.* Remember, you can't be angry or depressed or worried when you smile. And when you smile, other people like you.
- *Knowledge builds enthusiasm.* The more you know about something, the more enthusiastic you become.
- *Help others feel enthusiastic.* It makes you even more enthusiastic.

Chapter 8

Appeal to Others' Self-Interest to Achieve Your Goal

Recently, over a two-week period, a television station ran a series of public service commercials on colon cancer. With the cooperation of a local drugstore chain and a hospital, the station arranged for free tests, through the mail, to determine if a person showed signs of possible colon cancer. Amazingly, over 100,000 people went to drugstores, purchased a test kit, and mailed samples of their feces to the cooperating hospital. (More than 100 cases of colon cancer were discovered, making the effort extremely worthwhile.)

Now, during the same period, the same number of TV announcements were made urging people to contribute to the Red Cross. How many people responded with money or a pledge? Only 97. *The appeal to self-interest proved to be 1,000 times as powerful as the appeal to community interest.*

People are concerned about the needs of other people. But *they are motivated to action by their own needs.*

There is a law of human nature that cannot be dismissed. The law simply stated is: People are primarily interested in themselves, their family members, their job, their wealth, and their well-being. Interest in the welfare of others is second to interest in one's own welfare.

Intelligent advertisers pay attention to the law of self-interest. Notice how their messages always promise you or your loved ones more comfort, more safety, more status, better health, more enjoyment, a more attractive body, or more of various other benefits. The advertisers never tell you, "Buy our product so we can make more money."

A key to success is to put the interests of other people in *first* place and to keep your own interests in *second* place.

Keep your goal in focus. You want to influence people to buy from you, to give you their cooperation, to support your viewpoints, to work harder for you, to love you, to loan you money, or, in some other way, to help you.

Now, again with your goal in mind, remember other people are motivated by *their* self-interest. For example, people won't buy from you to help you earn a commission; they'll buy from you only if the purchase benefits them.

People want you to tell them:

- What's in it for *me*?
- How much will *I* make reselling the product?
- Exactly how will *I* benefit?
- Why should *I* work harder? How will *my* extra effort be rewarded?
- Suppose *I* take the job? What are *my* chances for promotion?

Telling the prospect how much money you will make if he or she buys can only hurt you. Do not mention how you will benefit from the help of another person. The gains you hope to make are not important. Concentrate *all* your energies on the benefits the other person will receive.

Put service to *others* first; money, promotions, status, job success, and other rewards will take care of themselves. But, should you put service to *yourself* first, life will be less rewarding.

Merchants who succeed ask continually, "How can I best serve the wants, needs, and desires of my customers?" Merchants who fail invariably ask, "How can I fool, deceive, overcharge or, in some other way, take advantage of the ignorance of my customers?"

Great salespeople concentrate on "How will my product help my prospect?" How much commission the salesperson will make is always a secondary consideration. Effective managers interpret company policies as beneficial to *employees,* not to themselves.

Physicians devoted to putting service to patients first, even though it means much self-sacrifice, build practices we admire.

Three easy ways to profit from appealing to the law of self-interest are to call people by name, to let others win the game of "Top It," and to give people pride.

CALL PEOPLE BY NAME

President Reagan often is referred to as the greatest communicator ever to serve as President. And for good reasons. He speaks slowly in a well-modulated voice, looks directly at the person or people he is speaking to, remains calm under pressure and uses simple, easy-to-understand words. Mr. Reagan employs many subtle but persuasive techniques in dealing with the public. Very importantly, at news conferences which are typically a very difficult presidential task, Mr. Reagan addresses reporters *by name* when accepting a question rather than just indicating with a hand motion which reporter may speak next. It may seem like a small point, but his method is conducive to helping create good relations with the press. Why? Because people cooperate better when they are recognized by name. Being addressed by name is a sincere and deeply appreciated compliment. It tells a person, "You are important to me."

Every person has a name and as Dale Carnegie observed, a person's name is the sweetest word in our language. People feel bigger and better when called by name because it is their most valuable possession. It gives them a sense of individuality — a feeling of being unique.

"Do you know who I am?" The law of self-interest — the tremendous craving for self-identity — comes through in many little ways. Recently, during only one week and on three separate occasions, three people revealed to me their enormous need to be recognized as an individual. After I made a presentation before a group of college administrators, one lady about 70 years of age lingered until I'd said hello to many well-wishers. It was obvious that she wanted to be the last person to speak to me. Finally, she was and I gave her a big "Hello!" She opened up by asking me very directly, "Do you know who I am?" Well, I meet hundreds of people every week and I'm not a memory expert. But in this case I did.

"Of course," I said. "You're Dr. Peg S."

Immediately her face lighted up. She was delighted that I remembered her name after ten years. Now here was a psychologist — someone you would think would be so self-assured she would not care whether or not people remembered her name. But she did. When I called her by name, I reassured her. I said, in effect, "You are important enough to be remembered after only a five-minute discussion ten years ago. You left a mark on me."

When we parted, she said to me, "Here is my card. Now if there is anything you can think of I can do for you, please call."

Later that same week, another woman indicated that great human need for recognition. She said to me, "Do you remember me?" She, too, wanted to believe she was important enough to have made a lasting impression on my mind. In this case, I had to say something off the top of my head — "I remember your face but your name slips my mind." I could see immediately a mixture of sadness and disappointment. I had offended her ego because I could not recall her name.

At another presentation, a man about 50 years of age came to the podium and opened up by saying, "I'll bet you don't remember me." At least this fellow gave me a chance to say something, such as "No, I don't, but let's get reacquainted right now."

The point: People everywhere want to be recognized by their names. Their names are their titles. The need to be remembered is an ego-need of the highest order. So, make a special effort to remember a person's name. Who would you rather do a favor — a person who says, "Ms. Thomas, will you help me?" or someone who says, "Lady, will you help me?"

Lyndon Johnson, the "Great Persuader," practiced remembering names, and Lyndon Johnson is the number one "persuader president" of modern times. He was enormously effective in bringing opposing factions together to get legislation passed.

Why was President Johnson so effective as a human relations engineer? He *worked* at it! Long before he succeeded Mr. Kennedy as President, he developed and practiced his own ten rules to make himself more effective in working with people.

President Johnson's system for how-to-win-influence-over-people appears below. *Note that he made "remember peoples' names" his first rule.*

> 1. Learn to remember names. Inefficiency at this point may indicate that your interest is not sufficiently outgoing.

2. Be a comfortable person so there is no strain in being with you. Be an old-shoe, old-hat kind of individual.
3. Acquire the quality of relaxed easy-going so that things do not ruffle you.
4. Don't be egotistical. Guard against the impression that you know it all.
5. Cultivate the quality of being interesting so people will get something of value from their association with you.
6. Study to get the "scratchy" elements out of your personality.
7. Sincerely attempt to heal every misunderstanding you have had or now have. Drain off your grievances.
8. Practice liking people until you learn to do so genuinely.
9. Never miss an opportunity to say a word of congratulation upon anyone's achievement, or express sympathy in sorrow or disappointment.
10. Give spiritual strength to people, and they will give genuine affection to you.

Here are five guidelines for calling people by their names to win their cooperation:

1. *Pronounce the other person's name correctly.* Nothing irritates a person more than to have his or her name mispronounced. Now it isn't always easy to pronounce a person's name the way he or she wants to hear it. We live in a culture made up of many different nationalities. So when you meet someone whose name you aren't sure you can pronounce the way the person wants to hear it, say something, such as "You have a distinguished name. Am I pronouncing it correctly?"

Usually, the other person will immediately repeat his or her name for you, letting you hear exactly how the person wants his or her name pronounced. Then to reinforce the person's name in your mind, use it as frequently as you can in the next few minutes of conversation.

2. *In conversation, use the other person's name often.* Do this and you fix the name in your memory, and you keep the positive attention of the person you're talking to.

Use the person's name often in written communications, too. Thanks to modern word-processing equipment, a person's name can easily be inserted in a letter. Here is an amazing fact. Companies who sell by direct mail have learned that even when people know the letter was prepared by a machine and the name was put in mechanically, response is better than if only the words "Dear Sir" or "Dear Madam" are used.

3. *Use nicknames only when you know they are preferred by the person.* I learned this lesson the hard way many years ago. I made a sales call on a fellow named James Gray. I immediately began calling him "Jim." I could sense as the interview developed that something was going wrong. "Jim" needed the service I was selling, and the price and other terms were right, but I didn't make the sale.

Later I learned why I had failed. "Jim" simply detested being called "Jim." He was extraordinarily proud that he had been named James after St. James in the Bible. James (now I have his name straight) once had explained to a friend of mine that no one ever refers to Saint James as Saint Jim.

Here's a suggestion. Call William "William," Elizabeth "Elizabeth," Peter "Peter," and Rebecca "Rebecca." If these people want to be called Bill, Liz, Pete, or Becky, they will tell you, "Please call me Bill," or whatever nickname they prefer. Never call a person by a nickname until the person asks you to.

4. *Use a person's last name until familiarity is established.* Undoubtedly, you've been turned off by telephone calls from strangers who immediately start calling you by your first name.

It shows sensitivity to call a person by his last name until he tells you to address him by his first name. Here's why: a) The person may resent it; b) he may feel you come on too strong (instead of breaking down the other person's defenses, you strengthen them); and c) first-naming it with strangers is not professional nor is it businesslike.

Remember, familiarity *still* breeds contempt.

5. *Spell the other person's name correctly.* Just as a person's ear is trained to reject his or her mispronounced name, a person's eye immediately picks up misspelling of his or her name. Today much of the mail we receive looks personal but isn't. Smart companies

make sure the people who put names into the computer spell them correctly. How do you feel when you receive mail with your name misspelled? You think to yourself, "If this company is so careless that it misspells my name, chances are it is equally careless about the quality of its merchandise, its prices, and its delivery dates."

A misspelled name on interoffice correspondence is even more devastating. It suggests inattention to detail.

LET THE OTHER PERSON BEAT YOU AT "TOP IT"

"Top It" is a game in which two people try to surpass each other in status, in money, in achievements, or in some other aspect of life. Here is an example.

Grandmother A shows some pictures of her grandson to grandmother B and says, "My grandson is going to enroll in the state university in September."

Grandmother B immediately counters, pulls out some pictures of her grandson, and says in an I'm-better-than-you voice, "Here is my grandson. He's been accepted at Harvard."

Grandmother B thinks she has won the "Top It" game because everybody "knows" Harvard is "better" than a state university.

Listen to conversations and you'll hear the "Top It" game played daily. On Monday morning, you'll hear people competing about who had the most way-out weekend, who caught the biggest fish, who attended the most lavish party, and who had the best seats at the football game. "Top It" is a favorite sport in offices, after-work get-togethers, on planes, at lunch — anywhere people meet.

The "Top It" game can produce bad results. A former associate of mine received an Excellent Teacher Award. A number of college officials were present at the ceremony, including my friend, the dean. Minutes after the ceremony, the dean complimented my friend, then said "When I was your age I had already received such-and-such award" (an award with even higher status).

The dean's comment irritated my friend (he's already related the incident to me three times!). The dean "won" the game of "Top It," but the professor he defeated soon moved to another university.

People don't like you when you beat them at the "Top It" game.

And if they don't like you, your chances of influencing them to cooperate with you, to buy from you, and to work harder for you are greatly reduced.

Here is how to deal effectively with "Top It."

1. *Know your objective and keep it in mind.* Are you talking with a person to make a sale or prove you're a better golfer than he? Do you want to get a job or let the interviewer know you went to a better school than she? In talking about grades with a child, do you want the kid to do better or do you want to put the youngster down by telling him you did even better when you were in school? In reviewing the day with your mate, do you want to let him or her get relieved of frustrations or do you want to talk about your problems?

2. *You display confidence when you avoid "Top It."* People who want to prove they are better than you are insecure and unsure.

Remember, someone who really has something to brag about doesn't have to brag!

Be a winner. Don't play "Top It."

There is only one way to win at "Top It." Don't play the game. Let the other person win by default. "Top It" is a kid's game (my bicycle is better than yours; my dad makes more money than your dad).

LET THE OTHER PERSON TALK

Here is a truth. People would rather talk about what interests them than hear you expound on what interests you. Put into sharper focus, people would rather talk about themselves, their interests, their families, their jobs, their problems, their hobbies, and their pets than listen to you tell stories about your interests.

One of the greatest compliments you can pay another person is to listen to him and to encourage him to talk and to confide in you.

Now, when you encourage others to talk about themselves, you reap a big harvest. The other person will view you as a friend, a great conversationalist (even if all you do is ask questions and comment very little on the answers), and someone he or she wants to get to know better.

It's not easy to let the other person do most of the talking. It's perfectly natural for you to want to tell what interests you. But again, keep in mind your objective: Am I conversing with this person to show how big my ego is or that I'm superior to him, or am I talking with Bob or Betty to win their support in achieving my goals? (Buy from me, work harder for me, or help achieve my objectives.)

GIVE PEOPLE PRIDE AND THEY'LL GIVE YOU 110 PERCENT

A friend of mine, Gus W., owns and manages a children's wear manufacturing company, employing about 300 people, in northern Georgia. The company is in its second century of operation and has never had a strike or work stoppage, and foreign competiton has dealt the American apparel industry a terrible blow. But Gus keeps on earning profits. Even though the work is routine and the pay scale is low, morale and productivity are high. How does Gus do it? Largely, by using "little" pride boosters. Gus tours the plant at least twice a week and says hello to each employee. He asks questions about their children and grandchildren, gives sympathy to those who may have experienced illnesses or deaths in their families, and makes inquiries about how he can help them — little expressions of thoughtfulness and kindness.

Last Christmas, Gus came up with a creative and enormously powerful motivational technique. He asked each employee to bring a covered dish to the Christmas party. Next, he asked each employee (95 percent are women) to submit her recipe for her covered dish.

Then Gus printed each person's recipe in an attractive cookbook which he later gave to every existing and prospective retail customer. The cookbook was a great pride-builder for the employees and the customers loved it!

The cookbook drew a lot of thank-you notes and they were prominently featured on bulletin boards.

Isn't that a wonderful way to build pride! And isn't it refreshing for customers to get a sincere gift from the company whose products they retail?

A construction manager in California told me, "Pride is the

most important tool we have. Without pride, everything ends up average or below average."

I asked him to explain because construction companies use a lot of expensive tools.

"Well," he began, "we don't have a lot of do's and don'ts for building morale among our employees. We just keep in mind all the time that pride is essential to our success and then we act on our pride-building ideas."

"Such as?" I asked.

"Little things. Before we begin a major project, we gather everyone together for a buffet. No long speeches — just a reminder that we are a great company and every person is important to the success of the project. Two or three times a summer, we go to a baseball game wearing T-shirts and caps with our logo. When we finish a building, we have a party followed by a paid holiday. When there's a parade in town we usually have a float."

"Sounds like your people have a lot of fun," I injected.

"We do have a lot of fun and it pays. You see, I don't have to worry about people being drunk or drugged up on the job, staying out sick when they aren't, or quitting to work for competition. And our workers don't steal each other's tools.

"You see, people want more than pay and fringes. They want to brag about what a great company they work for."

You often hear that the reason so many people lack pride in their company is that the organization has grown too large. This is nonsense. Individual pride does not have to decline simply because the organization gets big and employs thousands of people. Look at IBM, Delta, Disneyland and other top companies. Bigness does not destroy pride — only selfish, unthinking management does that.

The United States is the largest organization Americans belong to. And, despite the internal criticism that always exists, pride runs deep and morale is high.

Why? Because our traditions are remembered and passed down to new generations and newcomers. Sacrifices made by settlers, death, destruction and pain caused by wars, uncommon inventions, discoveries, and exploits all help remind people they are part of a great organization.

And pride — the all-powerful tool of successful living — is the result.

The point: Give people pride and you'll get 110 percent!

KIDS GIVE EVERYTHING THEY'VE GOT IN LITTLE LEAGUE FOR PRIDE — NOT MONEY

Last fall, I saw a championship soccer match between two teams of 11- and 12-year-olds. I've seen world series games, super bowls, major golf tournaments, and other extra-special sporting events. But this soccer game played by pre-teens beat all the professional sporting spectaculars I've seen in effort expended. Every kid on the field gave everything he had. Both teams had fought all season for the chance to play in the championship game. They had practiced for the game, exercised self-discipline, and even prayed to win.

Well, the Green team beat the Blue team 4 to 3. Now what did the Green team get for winning?

Fat cash bonuses? Of course not.

Professional soccer contracts? No.

Scholarships? No.

Gift certificates? No.

The Green team received an inexpensive trophy and a hamburger, Coke, and fries at McDonald's. The Blue team didn't receive a trophy, but they also got a special treat at the hamburger store.

I have never seen human beings of any age put more of themselves into an activity than those youngsters. And money was not involved.

The coaches gave up many Saturday mornings and evenings they could have spent golfing or jogging to teach the kids how to play. The mothers, too, sacrificed their time and energy to be sure there were plenty of sideline refreshments.

After the game, one of the referees and I watched the winning team celebrate, and the losing team, like real gentlemen, congratulated the winners. The referee, a successful builder, said to me, "You know, I've made a lot of money in my time, but I've never experienced a more satisfying Saturday morning in my life."

Next time you hear someone say something, such as "The way to solve this problem is to increase the pay," or "Money is the number one motivator," think. The key to turning people all the way on is through the heart or the spirit, not the pocketbook nor the bank account.

WHAT HAPPENS WHEN MANAGERS
DON'T FEED EGO/FOOD?

When people in an organization are never praised, never complimented, and are routinely criticized, negative results always occur. Look at these facts:

1. Employees steal more merchandise in retail stores than customers. Why? The main reason is employees, angry with the manager, want to "get even." And they do — by stealing.

2. Neglected employees are "sick" far more often than employees who are appreciated.

3. Turnover among employees who receive no spiritual motivation — only a paycheck — is much higher than turnover in organizations where spiritual motivation is stressed.

Keep in mind, sabotage and psychological terrorism is not confined to retail stores, offices, and factories. Professionals in hospitals, computer companies, airlines, and universities also get even when they feel unappreciated, exploited, and psychologically abused. In a university with which I am familiar, a departmental chairman drove away the five best professors in a department of ten by berating their work, oversupervising their activities, and using fear instead of praise.

The worst strikes, often prolonged and sometimes violent, occur in industries where managers fail to consider workers as people with strong and deep ego-needs. Managers in these industries typically regard employees with no more emotion than steel, cement, or some other commodity. And interestingly, most strikes take place in high-paying industries, indicating that the main cause of strikes is not money, but psychological neglect of employees' egos.

PUT-DOWN, "UNIMPORTANT" PEOPLE
DESTROY BUSINESS EVERYDAY

During the depths of a recession, I was in southern Florida to speak at a national convention. As soon as I arrived at the resort hotel where I had often stayed before, I sensed a decided change in the mood, the atmosphere of the place. The registration people were unusually slow, my room showed careless maid work, room service was inferior. The hotel just wasn't fun and first class like it had been.

Late the next morning, my purpose accomplished, I took the hotel limousine to the airport. I was the only passenger and I struck up a conversation with the young driver. I told him I was disappointed with the hotel. "It wasn't the hotel I remember from my last visit," I said.

Then the driver opened up. The hotel had changed management just a couple months ago and morale was down, he explained. Then he went on to relate some unhappy experiences. Two employees who work the front desk had been severely scolded for having spent $2.00 more for dinner one night than the manager of the hotel had authorized. The senior chef, who'd been there 12 years, was fired because the manager thought he was wasting food. Twenty-five percent of the maids were terminated and the workload of those remaining was increased proportionately. Room service, which had been a 24-hour-a-day operation, was available only to midnight.

"Worst of all," the driver continued, "the manager assembles the morning and afternoon shifts everyday and tells them how lousy they perform. There is no pride anymore. The only thing people look forward to is getting off work."

"Sounds like working at the hotel has gotten to be a pain," I said, "but at least you appear to be happy."

The driver laughed a little and said, "Sir, nothing could be further from the truth. This is my last week. I'm joining the staff at the hotel two blocks up the road."

"Why so?" I asked.

"Well, like most hotel people who work directly with the guests, I depend on tips for most of my income. Now, most guests I carry to the airport feel just like you. They're ticked off at the place when they leave and tip me less because of it. Besides, business is already falling off fast, so there are fewer passengers who need to catch a flight."

Flying home that day, I couldn't brush this incident from my mind. By bullying, cajoling, and abusing the "unimportant" people, the new hotel management was turning a fine, prosperous hotel into a loser.

Then I began to think of how other badly managed "unimportant" workers were destroying other businesses.

There were the automobile workers, who, although very well paid for generations, had been treated like machines; they decided to "get even" with their managers by making more mistakes, by producing sloppy workmanship, and by being absent as often as the contract allowed. In the process, they sent Americans shopping for foreign-made cars.

I thought also of "unimportant" garbage collectors who periodically make New York City smell like a dump and "unimportant" school teachers who strike. When you think about it, you'll notice that the "unimportants" in our society — the cashiers, receptionists, telephone operators, store clerks, police patrol personnel — the people on the front line — are unappreciated, are often abused, and are generally made to feel like nobodies, but they occupy, in one sense, the most important positions in society. *The "little" people meet the public and the public forms its impressions of a business by their behavior.* The public rarely sees the managers.

Personnel abuse is a cardinal management sin and it always leads to poor performance.

Low morale is caused by damage to the pride of "little" people in charge. Individuals who feel their pride is damaged or destroyed always find a way to fight back. Aboard ship in years past, fighting back was called mutiny. In industrial plants today, it is called a slow-down, a walk-out, or a wild-cat strike. In prisons, fighting back in extreme cases is called a riot. In offices, hospitals, universities, and other professional establishments, fighting back translates into high turnover, gossip, calling in sick, and plain goofing-off.

The message? Build people up, don't tear people down. Remember:

- Every person in an organization has an important job. If the job isn't important, eliminate it.
- Badger, punish, and abuse people and their performance goes down, never up.

Win or lose, a team develops pride when fans meet them at the airport. Auto workers take pride when one of them drives out the first new model. Actors feel better when a few of their professions are recognized with special awards. Nobel prizes and Pulitzer awards give encouragement to scientists and all creative people. Students need heroes and heroines to admire.

Everyone wants to be part of something important, big, good, and useful.

In a nutshell,

- To get what you want, put what other people want first. Show people how they will benefit, will earn more money, and will enjoy life, and *your* rewards come easily.
- A person's name is a person's most important identity.

Always:

    a) Pronounce the other person's name correctly.

    b) Use the other person's name often.

    c) Never use nicknames unless they are preferred.

    d) Address people by their last name until familiarity is established.

    e) Spell the other person's name correctly.

- Let other people beat you at the game of "Top It." Let people brag about what interests them; your objective is to influence the other person, not prove you are better than he or she.
- Give people pride and they will support you in what you want to do. Make others feel good about themselves and what they do.

Chapter 9

Five Sure Steps to Success Through Leadership

Here is an amazing fact: Eighty-three percent of today's millionaires were born in low- or middle-income families. Imagine! The great majority of successful people — corporate executives, entrepreneurs, lawyers, physicians, entertainers, members of legislative bodies, individuals at the top — *earned* their right to greatness.

Leadership is not for sale. Nor is it inherited, acquired by luck, or bestowed through marriage. And education correlates poorly, if at all, with leadership.

But leadership *can* be developed through persistent application. This chapter explains five simple, practical steps you can put to use immediately:

- Think excellence.
- Set winning examples.
- Speak up.
- Let other people help you.
- Take risks and win admiration.

STEP I: SUBSTITUTE "THINK EXCELLENCE" FOR "THINK AVERAGE" IN EVERYTHING YOU DO

Let me share with you an enormously important lesson — a principle that will help you gain success, wealth, and happiness.

To grasp this key concept, play this game in your mind. Imagine that you have just boarded a commercial airplane. You sit down, fasten your seat belt, and begin to relax. And then before take-off, you overhear the captain say to the crew, "You know, I'm uneasy about this flight. I don't think I can fly this plane very well. I'm just an average pilot."

What would you do? Chances are, you'd get off the plane as fast as possible. You knowingly will not trust your life to an average pilot.

Now carry this game a step farther. Assume you are in a hospital being prepared for an operation. As the anesthetic is taking effect, you hear the chief surgeon say to his or her associates, "I'm not sure I can do this operation. Sometimes I'm pretty good and sometimes I'm plain lousy at this procedure. You see, I'm only an average surgeon."

If it were possible, you'd get off the operating table immediately.

The point is, in matters of life or death, we don't want to put our lives in the hands of average physicians. And even if your life is not at stake, you don't want average people involved in your life in any way. Answer these questions:

Does your wife or husband want an average mate? Of course not. Your mate wants to love you and brag about you, not feel apologetic.

Do your kids want an average parent? Again, no. You are the most important element in the life of your youngster. For a child to think "My mom or dad is ordinary, mediocre" is tantamount to punishing a child.

Do your employees enjoy working for an average manager? No! At work, your people want to be proud of you and to believe their boss is great.

Should I be satisfied if I made an average income last year? Not really. An average income reminds you that you're only at the middle. One half of the people who work earn more than you!

Do I want an average C.P.A., lawyer, or financial consultant helping me with my monetary affairs? The answer to this question is a resounding *no*. We don't want people who help us manage our money to be only average.

The best definition I have heard of "average" — the definition that tells you how bad average is — is this: Average is the worst of the best and the best of the worst. There is nothing in the concept of average to suggest superiority or greatness. Average means only OK, so-so, mediocre, ordinary, or barely acceptable.

We define "excellence" — the quality success-minded people

seek in everything they do — as nearly perfect, unusually good, the best possible.

Thinking average holds people back because it makes them feel secure and complacent. Students feel safe when they can say, "I scored average, so I'm OK." Plant managers feel comfortable when they can report, "We were average in productivity compared to the industry." And many sales managers think they've done an acceptable job when they've reached their sales quotas. But excellence is not merely reaching a quota. Excellence is exceeding the goal, giving better service than is required, delivering our best efforts to whatever we are doing — working, rearing children, playing games, or managing others.

Professionals in every field strive for excellence, and they are constructively unhappy with themselves when results are less than excellent. The coach who loses as many games as he wins is unhappy with his performance. So is the entertainer who receives only modest applause. And the manager who delivers results no better than last year is dissatisfied with himself.

You see, professionals are committed to excellence. The winners in life practice the wisdom in the old saying, "If something is worth doing, it is worth doing well."

Many so-called "reasons" have been given to explain why productivity in the United States fell behind other nations in the free world over the past 20 years. These reasons — they really are excuses — include decline in the work ethic, high energy costs, the welfare system, high interest rates, foreign competition, and many more. But these excuses don't really explain why hundreds of thousands of businesses went bankrupt, why millions were unemployed, and why a large segment of society is disillusioned and discouraged.

The underlying reason for economic turmoil and the social problems it created is our national obsession with thinking average, instead of thinking excellence. Evidences of average thinking are everywhere. Look at these examples:

Production Worker: "The union contract calls for six units per hour. That's what I produce. Why should I beat the standard or average? Besides, the union boss loves me when I do only what the law (the contract) requires."

Bureaucrat: "I'm safe in my job. Why should I do more than the minimum expected of me?"

Executive: "I've had a good year. We equaled the average profit performance for the industry."

Student: "I got a C-average last quarter. That's not bad because it means I passed."

Few people put forth the second effort in what they do. That helps explain why few enjoy the really good life.

SHOW COURAGE — THINK EXCELLENCE

You know people who take refuge in being average because they are afraid to compete. These people reason, "In my present job I'm about equal to everyone else. If I left this safe place, I might not be able to cut it and, instead of being average, I'd be below average or even fail."

Let me explain how the fear of bigger, more challenging assignments works.

I knew Leslie R. as a very bright student. He went to a state university where he majored in TV and radio communications. Leslie was offered a number of jobs with TV stations when he graduated. The offer he accepted was in his home town, a city of about 75,000 people. I met Leslie 25 years later when I visited his city to talk to the chamber of commerce. I spent an hour with him, listening to him unburden himself about his dissatisfaction with following a safe but average mediocre career.

"You know," Leslie began, "for the first few years after I joined my home town station, I was offered better paying, more prestigious TV assignments. But I always turned them down."

"Why?" I asked.

"Oh, I had all sorts of reasons," Leslie replied. "I felt I needed more experience before I moved up to a bigger assignment. Or I preferred my multi-level job — doing the news, the sports, and the weather. But looking back, I have to confess, those were only excuses. Now that I'm much older and most of my TV career is behind me, I have to admit the real reason I didn't accept one of those good offers was fear. In my assignment here, I knew I was pretty good. But I was plain afraid I couldn't cut it in a faster-paced, more demanding environment. In the best stations, you have to be truly superior to keep your job. But I'm one of those guys who thinks he's only average. So I played it safe and stayed here.

"My big regret," Leslie continued, "is my lack of confidence. Believe me, the saddest words of tongue or pen really are, 'it might have been.' "

I know a Leslie-type surgeon — a brilliant fellow who avoided practicing in several of the nation's best hospitals because he was psychologically crippled by the "I'm-only-average" syndrome. As I've traveled the nation, I've come to know coaches who could have been great, musicians who could have won fame and fortune, individuals who could have succeeded in their own business, managers who might have become CEO's, and excellent professors who, too, kept their light under a bushel — all because they were trapped into thinking, "I'm only average."

The point: Each of us is controlled by the way we think. To enjoy the best this life offers, refuse to let mediocrity control what you do. Compete with yourself. Think excellence.

Cynics tell us God must love common or average people because he made so many of them. But positive-minded, success-oriented people say God doesn't like average people because he made everyone unique and special in some way. Because each person is unique, each person was designed to be a world champion at something.

REWARD PEOPLE WHO THINK EXCELLENCE — REMOVE THOSE WHO THINK AVERAGE

During the lowest point of the last recession, I had lunch in the Los Angeles airport prior to flying to Chicago. The service in the restaurant was abominable. My waitress was rude, crude, and insulting. She brought me something I didn't order, glowered at me, and made me feel like I was really messing up her life. Even when she brought me the check, she was not the least bit pleasant. She simply said with ice in her voice, "I expect a 20 percent tip." (Needless to say, I was not going to tip this person. The main reason service is so bad in so many restaurants is that customers feel intimidated and think they must tip. In my view, a gratuity should never be given for unsatisfactory service.)

As I exited and paid my check, I said to the manager, "Why on earth do you have that waitress working for you? One hundred thousand people here in Los Angeles are out of work! Is she the best you can find?" Angry, I left without waiting for a reply and headed for my flight.

Once aboard the plane, I soon was joined by a seat companion. In a few minutes he said to me, "I saw what happened in the restaurant and overheard your remark to the manager, and I agree. I had the same waitress and she was about as bad as they come. But I didn't quite get your point about one hundred thousand people in Los Angeles being out of work and why that waitress still had a job. Maybe she has seniority. Or maybe she has a couple of kids to feed and no husband or a husband out of work."

I couldn't resist telling my seat companion that I truly believe all things work together for good. There is even a good side to a recession.

My companion said to me, "How anyone can see anything good in a recession is beyond me. I run a catalog house in Chicago and everything connected with the recession has hurt my business. There is nothing 'good' about times like these. If you see any benefits from what we call in Chicago a depression, tell me."

"Well," I began, "one of my enterprises is growing pine trees in the Southeast. About once every decade we have a pretty bad ice storm. Now, the negative side of the icy conditions is downed power lines, ice on the roads, some families without heat for a couple days — things like that.

"But on the positive side, the ice serves to prune the trees. Dead or sick trees fall and weak limbs are brought down. The net result is that after the ice is gone, tree farmers have healthier forests."

"I can understand that," my companion said, "but how does that example relate to an economic recession?"

I said to this fellow, "Let me explain. A recession, like an ice storm, signals a time to prune the organization — to remove people who aren't carrying their share of the load."

"Well," my friend interrupted, "I have three hundred employees and I'm going to have to let fifty of them go by the end of the month. But I'm going to use seniority as my guide to decide who goes and who stays."

"It's your business," I observed, "but if you want to have a stronger, healthier, go-get-'em organization when the recession is over, you'll use present conditions to prune your work force. It's never fun to remove people, but when you have no choice, it's smart to keep your most productive people."

About six months later, I got a phone call from my seat companion. He told me that after a lot of thought he decided to release workers based on their performance, not on their seniority. It was a tough decision, he said, but it was also the right decision.

"You may recall I had to remove fifty people," he explained. "But the amazing thing is, we now do the same work with two hundred fifty employees as we did with three hundred.

"I learned a big lesson," my friend continued. "We are obsessed in our society with providing employment, not getting the job done."

Tomorrow, when you visit offices or go to the post office, stop and ask yourself how more efficient and less costly services and products would be if organizations stopped tolerating average, mediocre, I-don't-care performers.

The point: Bet on people who strive for excellence, not on those who are second-rate performers.

Remember, average is the best of the worst and the worst of the best. As you fashion a better, richer, more satisfying life, keep three points in mind.

First, *strive for excellence in everything you do.* See the wisdom in the old saying "If something is worth doing, it's worth doing well." All work is important and should be performed in the best manner possible. Remember, you'll make more money when you are an excellent performer. And you'll enjoy more satisfaction which is the source of the real wealth you seek.

Second, *detest thinking average.* Thinking average will never help you realize your dreams. No kid likes to say, "My dad is an average dad." No boss wants to tell his superior, "Joe is only an average salesman," and no one will ever brag about you if you look, think, talk, and act as an average person does.

Third, *look forward to competing with the best.* You'll never know how good you are until you match yourself against a big challenge.

Mediocre people want company. They delight in seeing others sink to their level. Deny them their devilish delight. Don't let average associates pull you down to their performance level. Get your advice from winners. Model your behavior after the best. Keep moving toward excellence and enjoy the rewards.

STEP II: SET WINNING EXAMPLES

Ask someone, "How did you learn to speak our language?" And he or she will likely say, "From my parents." But one's parents are the source, not the method, by which we learn to speak. Simply said, we learn our language by copying and imitating other people.

Chances are, your friends who happen to be Catholic, Protestant, Jewish, Buddhist, or Moslem had parents of the same faith. Even for most of us, our politics are the political beliefs of our parents.

Most people acquire their attitudes toward religion, politics, economics, marriage, discipline, work, and sex by copying the examples set by parents, teachers, superiors, and peers.

Leadership is example setting. Over time, the philosophy and habits of the person in charge become the philosophy and habits of the support group or followers.

At least 90 percent of a person's behavior can be traced to the examples he or she copies from other people. Setting the right examples, then, is an essential part of being a winning leader.

SELECT YOUR ROLE MODEL CAREFULLY

An advertising executive told me about an experience that put him on the right track in dealing with people.

"I was twenty-two at the time, fresh out of college, when I learned a profound lesson. I got a job with an advertising agency as an assistant to an account executive. My boss, Bill, was short-tempered, had little patience with the artists, copywriters, and other creative people. He'd snap at them, often ridicule their ideas, and put them down.

"Now this was my first job. I didn't like the way he handled people, but I assumed it was the right way. After all, he was the account executive and his way must be the right way.

"One Friday I was out of the office on agency business. When I returned, I had a message telling me to see Mr. Campbell, the senior vice-president.

"Mr. Campbell got right to the point. 'Bill, we've just let Phillips (my boss) go.' The only explanation Mr. Campbell gave was 'Phillips had difficulty getting cooperation from the creative people.' Then Mr. Campbell said, 'You are welcome to stay on. Please report to Jack Brown.'

"I discovered Jack was a direct opposite of Bill. Jack made the creative people feel needed and important. He was consistently polite and understanding. We accomplished a great deal and produced one successful campaign after another.

"I often wonder," my friend mused, "what would have happened to me if I had served a year or two under Bill. Looking back, I was young, inexperienced, and very impressionable. Had I acquired Bill's habits, I would likely have become a failure. But as if a divine hand were watching over me, I got the opportunity to work with Jack. He became my role model and it's really paid off."

My friend's experience teaches two big lessons:

- As you move up the ladder, keep asking yourself, "Am I setting a good, positive example for my support people?" Remember, treat company property and money as if it were your own and your people will, too. Give 100 percent of your effort and so will your followers. Speak well of your company and so will those you lead.
- Select the right model for your behavior. Before taking a job, ask yourself, "Would I be satisfied with myself if I developed the habits and attitudes of the person I would report to?"

MAKE SURE YOUR CHILDREN LEARN GOOD EXAMPLES

Last fall there were teachers' strikes in many parts of the nation. Some of them were negative and bitter. Teachers carried pickets with messages such as "Hang the School Board," "We Babysit for

You, Pay Us," and "Stop Exploitation of Teachers."

This commotion by teachers bothered me. One of the key principles education should teach is respect for authority. The striking teachers' absolute defiance of the school board's authority would make a lasting impression on the minds of the students. Why should they respect authority when the people whom they are supposed to admire — the teachers — thumb their noses at it?

A mother in one of the school districts where the strike had been going on for over a month talked to me about her problem. "My husband and I are really upset. Our two kids are being deprived of an education. It's not fair."

"I agree it's not fair," I said, "but there is something you can do about it. Send them to a private school."

"Oh, Jim and I have thought about it, but we can't afford a private school. Besides, we're paying school taxes."

My reply was quick and direct, "I know it may place a financial strain on you and I know it's unfair having to pay for both a private school and a public school. But you owe it to your kids to give them the best. Sell one of your cars, refinance your home, eat cheaper food. Do whatever it takes to get your kids into a school where teachers set a good example."

I also pointed out how bad it is for their children to be exposed to teachers who were so petty they refused to teach because of a few percentage points in pay scales. I reminded my friend that if the teachers harbored such negative feelings on the issue of pay, what other deplorable examples were they setting for your children.

The problems of our public school system will never be solved with higher pay for teachers. The solution lies in selecting teachers who are dedicated to helping children learn. The appeal of teaching, like the ministry, has never been and should never be the monetary reward. The opportunity to help young minds grow and develop a sound set of values toward home, other people, and the nation should be what attracts people to the teaching profession.

My friend got the point. Three days later, her children were in a private school.

The old saying "Actions speak louder than words" has not been discarded. What we do, the way we act and react, and how we respond to situations teach children far more than the words we speak. Look at these facts:

Statistical evidence shows unmistakenly that children with an alcoholic parent or parents are far more likely to have drinking problems than children whose parents do not drink or drink only moderately. Children see, children do.

Parents who physically abuse their children were themselves abused when they were children. If youngsters are abused, when they grow up, they reason it's their turn to abuse.

Most adults in poverty experienced poverty as children. Millions of adult Americans, having lived all their lives in poverty, regard it as the norm. The example of poverty often teaches poverty.

Most adult Americans who attend church attended church when they were children. The converse is true. Most adults who do not go to church did not attend church when they were young.

Fathers who abandon their children usually are sons of fathers who abandoned their children.

Children of parents who believe in and support a labor union (not the company that pays them) are more likely to support unions than children of parents who saw the company (not a union) as their true benefactor.

One way or another, consciously or subconsciously, the habits, viewpoints, and prejudices of parents become models for the behavior of their offspring. The message: Most of your child training is by example, not words. So, make your examples positive and constructive.

Look at it this way. You teach a child to walk by your example of walking (notice how a little boy tries to walk like his daddy); you teach children how to use a spoon, knife and fork — not by the lecture method, but by the example method. Use of seat belts is demonstrated when you wear your seat belt, not by a discourse on safety to a four-year-old.

Much of a child's life is programmed by the time he is three years old. And almost none of that programming was put into his mind with verbal symbols. Our lives then are shaped by the examples of others.

Recently I made a presentation for one of the nation's leading department store chains. It was a special event for me because I had known my host, the chairman of the company, 25 years ago when he was a stock clerk just beginning his retailing career.

"You've come a long way," I told my friend, "and you can be mighty proud of what you've done. I knew you had the right stuff. But you must have done something special, something extra special, to make it all the way to chairman."

My friend laughed and said, "I did develop one management concept you taught me. It's paid off more than anything else."

Now he had my curiosity aroused, so I asked, "What was that?"

"Just this. You made all of us trainees memorize the little verse, 'What kind of a world would our world be if everyone in it behaved like me?' Well, I've lived by that verse ever since. Now it's 'What kind of a store would our store be if every manager were just like me?' And it's worked wonders in my career and the hundreds of managers who are accountable to me. Every manager in our company is taught to train his or her people by setting good examples."

"Any kind of examples in particular?" I asked.

"I concentrate on three areas," he replied.

"First is the 'customer care' example. All of our managers spend some time everyday working with customers. This helps the employees. After all, the best way by far to train people how to sell is to show them how to sell. And it's great for employees' morale when they see managers, and I mean all managers, including myself, showing merchandise, handling a credit problem, wrapping a package, or doing any task. It's good for our managers because they get a day-by-day feel for the business.

"Now the second example," my CEO friend went on, "is the 'resource respect' example. That means show respect for our merchandise, money, fixtures, and equipment. When a manager treats merchandise carefully and arranges it properly, employees will, too. One good example about how to make merchandise look appealing is worth more than a four-page memo!"

"What's the third example?" I asked.

"I call it the 'professional look' example," my friend replied. "It's important that our people look like intelligent professional people. Our managers establish a dress code by projecting a professional look — neat, clean, and conservative."

"You put a lot of faith into building a merchandising team by setting the examples you want followed," I observed.

"I sure do," the executive replied. "It's the only way, in my opinion, to build the right attitudes and skills. There is no way I can teach you how to tie your shoes except by showing you how to tie your shoes. And there is no way to teach a person how to serve a customer except by demonstrating how to serve a customer."

STEP III: SPEAK UP

Leading is speaking. Leaders speak up. Consider some of the great leaders.

Churchill was a master at speaking. Roosevelt was an excellent speaker. Martin Luther King, Jr. could hold tens of thousands of people spellbound. Adolph Hitler, while a devil of the worst sort, was a leader, nevertheless. In his book *Mein Kampf,* he explains the importance of speaking as it relates to leadership. He said, "I know that one is able to win people far more by the spoken word than by the written word, and that every great movement on this globe owes its rise to the great speakers and not to the great writers."

In business, it's the people who voluntarily speak at conferences and meetings (not the memo writers) who move up to more responsibilities. But few people have the confidence to express their views. I had lunch recently with a friend who is chairman of a growing company. He told me, "I have a problem. There are fifteen directors on my board. We meet four times a year. But only three or four of the directors say anything. To get the others to talk, I have to direct a specific question at them individually as, 'John, what do you think about this or that?' "

I assured my friend that lack of participation is typical in all meetings. I pointed out that anytime you have 10 to 20 people together, only about 25 percent will volunteer any comments at all. The other 75 percent just sit there.

I gave my friend another observation. "The silent ones at the meeting will do their talking afterwards in groups of two or three. People who have no comment during a formal meeting always have plenty to say after the meeting in offices, at lunch, or after work."

Recall the last meeting you attended — maybe a meeting of managers, of salespeople, or of members of a club. Probably only a few said anything. And it is very likely, after the meeting the quiet ones paired off in groups of two or three and made comments, such as "I wish someone had suggested...," or "Why didn't anyone tell the boss about the problem we're having with the new security system?" or "I wish someone had said something about...."

One word explains why most people don't speak up: *Fear.* Fear of ridicule. Fear of looking foolish. Fear of saying something controversial. Fear of one's imagined shortcomings keeps people silent. It takes courage and confidence to say something in public.

Some people believe the old proverb "It's better to be silent and thought a fool than open your mouth and prove it." But the proverb misleads. Practice silence, and you greatly reduce your chances of gaining influence.

No other qualification for success is as important as the ability to speak to other people, to command their attention, and to win them to your point of view.

Our educational system generally ignores this requirement for success. One can earn a Ph.D. in dozens of fields, including business administration, and never receive any instruction in speaking. Meanwhile, it is virtually certain you cannot make it to the top in your field or even come close unless you learn how to express yourself positively. Here are six guidelines that will help you get the speak-up habit.

1. *Speak up. Raise a question, express an opinion, volunteer a personal experience or, in some other way, say something at every meeting you attend.* Speak up and you begin to stand out. You divorce yourself from the 75 percent who say nothing except to murmur a "yes," "no," "I-don't-know," "Sounds-OK-to-me" comment when asked a direct question. The people who chair meetings are looking for ideas, suggestions, and helpful comments. Volunteer your views and you exhibit leadership talent which will be rewarded. Tell yourself, "I will say something at every meeting I attend." It won't be easy. But remember, the only way to conquer the fear of speaking is to speak.

2. *Express your comments positively.* Don't weaken what you say by prefacing it with a remark, such as "I've got an idea. It probably won't work, but...." Never cheapen your suggestion before you make it. Would you buy a car from a salesperson who said, "You probably won't like this car, but go ahead and look at it, anyway?"

3. *Communicate honestly.* When Churchill talked to the British people during World War II, he told them the truth. He promised blood, sweat, toil, and tears would be needed to win. Great corporate leaders directing companies in trouble promise, "The road to recovery will be difficult."

Some would-be leaders promise the easy road to success. But, people respond best to the truth. A football coach who tells his team that "winning this game will be like eating cake" is certain to have trouble.

Once you lose credibility, once people feel you aren't telling the truth, they lose faith in everything else you say — even the truth. In World War I, German soldiers were told that the British soldiers were sissys and the French troops had their minds on only women and wine. When the German soldiers met the French and British in combat, they soon learned that the propaganda from the home front wasn't true. Soon they wouldn't believe anything they were told.

During the last recession, many companies asked their workers to take pay cuts to help the organization survive. Those companies that laid the facts on the bargaining table had less problems getting employees to accept a pay cut or a shortened work week. But companies that tried to fool their workers by misinterpreting financial data faced real problems.

The point: Tell people the truth and they will support you. Tell lies and people will desert you.

Teachers: If the exam that your students will take next week is difficult, tell them the truth and they will be better prepared.

Supervisors: If some unwanted overtime is required, tell the employees why the extra work is absolutely necessary and they will cooperate.

Executives: If the company is in financial trouble, tell the shareholders and directors the truth and they will support your plans for financial recovery. Lie to them and their resentment of you will build and they may ask you to leave.

Parents: You're exercising leadership when you let your children know that achieving anything worthwhile demands application, persistence, and sacrifice.

4. *Deal with criticism positively.* No one enjoys being criticized or laughed at. It's humiliating to make mistakes in public. The big fear of appearing foolish includes all kinds of little fears — making mistakes in pronunciation and grammar, forgetting what one wants to say, offending someone, and being told later what we did wrong.

Everyone dislikes criticism. The way to handle criticism is to expect criticism. Accept it as a compliment. Remember, the most criticized person in America is not a terrorist or an enemy of the people. The person who attracts the most flak is the President. Not only do some columnists disparage whatever the President says, he is also lambasted by ignorant and shiftless people who find fault with him because he is not giving them something for nothing.

In business, no one is critical of the janitor, but lots of people find fault with what the chairman of the board says and does.

So, be glad you're being criticized. It's proof you are growing. It takes strength to be on the firing line, so take pride.

5. *Inform and inspire, but never attack.* The presentation that gets positive results is a good blend of information and inspiration. A good speech never attacks someone else's ideas. Regardless of what another speaker may have said that is contrary to your views, don't attack and try to prove why he or she is wrong.

It pays to be constructive. An advertising executive told me how his agency won a multi-million dollar beverage account.

"Three other agencies were invited to present their campaign ideas. The client had told me what their plans were. He said to me, 'Feel free to be critical of their strategies if you feel doing so helps put across your plans.' "

"Did you?" I asked.

"Absolutely not," my friend replied. "I simply said at the beginning of my presentation, 'The other agencies you're considering employ fine, creative people. But our strategy is unique, so I won't compare what we will do with what they would do." Then I proceeded to describe my plan. My presentation was in a class by itself. Had I tried to prove why we were the best agency, I would have opened the door to an argument. By refusing to attack my competitors, I avoided conflict and got the account."

Remember, small-minded people fight with their fists and clubs. The petty-minded people who are just a notch above them fight with their mouths, and truly big-minded people don't fight at all.

When you say your plan (platform or approach or strategy) is better than someone else's or when you attack, some of the decision-makers will rally in support of your competitor. Instead, simply explain your plan positively and conscientiously without putting down your competitors. Never, absolutely never, use the platform to put down someone else. It only leads to a war you'll probably lose.

President Reagan's re-election campaign in 1984 is a classic example of how to deal with competition. The President never even mentioned his competitor by name! Mr. Reagan did not run against someone; he concentrated his energies running *for* a positive program. And he received a record number of votes.

In selling anything — ideas or products — concentrate 100 percent of your effort on what is good about what you offer. Never attack your competitor's ideas or products. Television commercials that show how product A is better than product B and C simply give free plugs for products B and C.

6. *Speak Simply.* Confucius said, "A great person never loses the simplicity of a child." Ralph Waldo Emerson observed, "Nothing is more simple than greatness. Indeed, to be simple is to be great." Just as a machine should have no unnecessary parts, what you say should have no unnecessary words.

Look at these common expressions:

Bad Form	Better Form
The undersigned	I
At the present time	Now or Today
At the earliest possible moment	Soon
Allow me to express my appreciation	Thank you
The writer thinks that	I think

At a later date	Later
In the neighborhood of	About
In view of the fact that	Because
Subsequent to	After
Without further delay	Immediately

Big words, complex ideas, long drawn-out statements make you come across as stiff, pompous. Instead, speak simply — so a child understands what you are saying. Never use the podium to show off how smart and educated you are.

Apply Emerson's commandment, *be simple* in everything you do. Olympic diving champions use no unnecessary muscles in performing a complicated dive; magicians perform their deceptions so simply every child feels he or she "can do it, too." Award-winning actors work tremendously hard so they don't appear to be acting.

STEP IV: LET OTHER PEOPLE HELP YOU

The head of an electronics company in California related how he used what's called participative management to advance his career. His experience says a lot about leading others.

"My first assignment after graduating from the naval academy was service as a junior electronics officer aboard an aircraft carrier. Immediately, I realized I knew very little about the technical work. But I quickly recognized I had several thoroughly experienced petty officers. So, everyday I would bring them together, outline our activities for the day, and then ask them for their ideas on how to proceed. Their response was terrific. Later, I learned the junior officer they previously reported to never asked for their opinions. They loved my participative style.

"After my release from the Navy, I went to work for an electronics company. Again, I soon realized how much I needed the ideas and skills of my support people. Again, I discovered letting them help plan activities guaranteed that the work would get done and done well.

"Promotion followed rapidly. I was made president of the company two years ago when I was thirty seven. I attribute my success to one leadership quality — to inspire people by letting them participate in the thinking and planning."

Here are the guidelines to get other people to help you.

1. *Regard praise as money. Invest it.* Leaders never hog glory. A leader who receives praise always invests it in his or her supporters. A smart football coach never takes credit for a victory. He gives the credit to the team. This makes the team want to try even harder next week. So, when you are congratulated or receive an award, always take the praise you receive and reinvest it to enlarge the morale of your supporters. If you're a sales manager and sales go up, don't take the credit. Give it to your salespeople. If you're a production manager and you exceed your goal, praise the workers. Get more mileage from the praise you receive.

Leaders never hog glory. Just as money invested wisely will make more money, praise invested in the people who help you will get them to do even better.

2. *Take 100 percent responsibility when things go wrong.* A leader understands clearly that you can delegate authority or power to act but you cannot delegate responsibility for the result.

In 1984, 312 marines were killed by a terrorist in Beirut. President Reagan, as commander-in-chief, acted wisely and took full responsibility for the tragedy. Had he blamed the Commandant of the Marine Corps, he would not have acted as leader. And the President would have come under severe attack.

The Bay of Pigs was a disaster. Some of President Kennedy's aides urged him to blame the Eisenhower administration for the failure since much of the planning was done before Mr. Kennedy was President. But Mr. Kennedy exercised leadership and told the American public, "I take full responsibility." After that, criticism of the failure decreased greatly.

President Nixon violated the responsibility law during the Watergate affair and had to resign or be impeached. Many believe if Mr. Nixon had taken full responsibility — had he said to the American people, "I accept responsibility for the break-in and dirty tricks" — his presidency would have been saved. But, stubbornly, he tried to blame others and history will remember him only for his faults, not for the good things he accomplished.

When things go wrong, never put the blame on your support people. It makes you look small and weak. Instead, act big. Admit that you, not your people, goofed. Act big and you'll prove you are a leader.

3. *Coordinate the minds of other people.* Great leaders study people. And people-knowledge is the most important information you need to achieve success, wealth, and happiness. Job-knowledge is not. Because you can program a computer doesn't mean you can run the department. You may know how to sell but still be unqualified to be sales manager. And a person may have earned a 4.0 grade point in school and not be a leader.

You see, knowledge itself is not power. It is the raw material of power and needs to be channeled. Chances are, you know exceptionally well-informed people who couldn't lead a Boy Scout troop or serve as an effective president of a civic club. Leadership is tapping, coordinating, and meshing the knowledge of other people.

Again, leadership is people-knowledge, not task- or job-knowledge.

Consider this example. Assume you want to become president of a great university. To prepare yourself, you decide to take every course the university teaches. Do this and you'll be at least 2,500 years old before your preparation is complete.

Or suppose your goal is to become CEO of General Motors. To get ready for the top post, you decide to master every job performed at G.M. Again, you'd be at least 2,500 years old before you would be ready.

Leaders must be able to manage people who know far more specialized knowledge than they do.

To become an effective leader, concentrate on studying people — how to motivate them to cooperate, to put forth their best effort, and to make personal sacrifices.

STEP V: TAKE RISKS AND WIN ADMIRATION

A few years ago, on a short flight from Cleveland to Columbus, my seat companion was the extraordinary Christian philosopher, Dr. Robert Schuller. He made a provocative comment that contains a great leadership lesson. He said, "Why is it when most people part company they say, 'Take care'? Our nation is built by people who take risks, not by those who take care. Converting possibilities into realities always requires risk."

What an important leadership concept! Every business is started by someone who takes risks. And to make a new business succeed requires taking more and more risks. Will people like our products? Will employees work out? Will our investment pay off? These are a few of the risk-related questions entrepreneurs face.

All great achievements are made by risk-takers. Dr. Christian Barnard risked his reputation as a surgeon when he did the first transplant of a human heart. Lee Iacocca took enormous risks in his successful attempt to revive the Chrysler Corporation. And Dr. Norman Vincent Peale risked being dismissed from the clergy when he authored the world-changing book *The Power of Positive Thinking.*

Education, unfortunately, concentrates on how to avoid risks, not on how to profit from taking risks. Our business schools turn out five corporate hired hands for each risk-taking entrepreneur. And by my own first-hand observation, five times as much effort is given by professors to risk-avoidance as is devoted to successes in spite of risks.

A football coach explained why he decided to use a play that cost his team both a tie and the conference championship. "We scored a touchdown with less than thirty seconds to play. That score put us within one point of the other team. Now I had to make the biggest decision of the season: Do we go for an almost certain one-point play, which would have given us a tie and the conference championship, or do we try the much riskier two-point play? If the two-point play didn't work, we'd lose the game *and* the conference title!"

"As I recall the game, you tried the two-point play," I injected.

"Yes, and it failed, so we lost," the coach continued, "but I don't regret it. Just before the play that failed, we called a time-out and the quarterback said to me, 'Everyone out there wants us to try for two points. We came here to win!'

"I took a lot of criticism about the decision that cost us a tie and the championship. Thousands of fans were unhappy. But each player was glad we took the chance. And as a coach, I've always put the players first — it's their lives I'm trying to build.

"We played that game thirteen years ago and many times over

the years the young men who played that day have told me it was the greatest lesson they ever learned. It helped them understand what courage means."

Keep track of how often you hear someone say, "I wish I had invested in the XYZ company," or "I wish I had gotten a job with the ABC corporation," or "I wish I had done such and such." And the "I-wish-I-had-but-didn't" people are an unhappy lot.

Yet everyone who achieves success, wealth, and happiness takes more risk than his or her counterpart who elects to live in mediocrity. Taking risks helps you discover how good you are.

Remember, nothing ventured, nothing gained. An amateur writer told me, "Oh, I've never submitted anything to a publisher. It would probably be rejected." A young man explained why he didn't go into selling. "I don't think I have what it takes." He didn't risk trying. Many people explain why they didn't change jobs this way: A job change means risk, uncertainty.

Risk-taking does not mean gambling. When you take a risk you have some control over the outcome. When you gamble, the result is out of your hands.

Recently I met Jack W. in Detroit. Jack had worked for 17 years as an engineer with General Motors. "My job was OK but I couldn't put one hundred percent of myself into it. I had thought for years about going into business for myself. But I always found a good reason why I couldn't — not enough money, I might fail, my family and I needed a sure source of income — excuses such as these. Finally, my wife told me to take the plunge. 'You're not happy.' She reassured me that I could make it. So, I quit and set up my own engineering company. For two years, I was the entire staff and sold my services to companies wanting custom-outfitted vans and recreational vehicles. I'm doing very well now."

I complimented him for having the courage to give up certainty for uncertainty.

"But there is more of my experience I want to share with you," Jack continued, "I had new pride in myself, new confidence. I really felt better about myself. But another benefit was greater respect from my wife, kids, and friends. People admired me for taking the plunge and going on my own."

People who make it know their priorities. They put risk-taking first and security second. They know that risk-taking, persistently, creatively, and intelligently applied, will in time provide as much security as anyone wants.

To lead, put these principles to work:

- Think excellence. Great satisfaction comes from doing your best in every activity. Average performance is never good enough.
- You are being copied by others in everything you do. So, set the kind of examples you want followed.
- Speaking up is essential to leadership. Express yourself at every opportunity. Conquer fear by speaking up.
- You need other people to help you achieve your goals. So, win their cooperation.
- Invest all the praise you receive.
- Take 100 percent responsibility when things go wrong.
- Coordinate the knowledge of other people.
- Have the courage to take risks. Taking risks is as essential to success as breathing is to life.

Chapter 10

Five Never-to-Be-Forgotten
Keys to Success and Wealth

In the next 24 hours, 219 Americans will become millionaires. In only 30 days, 6,570 people will have joined the ranks of the financially free. In the next 12 months, the number of millionaires will swell by about 80,000, and over the next decade by about 800,000 people. Ten years from now, one household in every 64 will enjoy millionaire status.

These projections are based on 12 years of intensive research by Dr. Thomas Stanley, the foremost expert on wealthy people and how they get rich.

The new millionaires come from the lowest to the highest social classes, the worst and the best educational backgrounds. Some are physically weak, others are strong and healthy. The one quality all new millionaires have in common is a dream of success, wealth, and happiness which they deliberately work hard to make happen. Successful people are dreamers who act out their fantasies. Millionaires are ordinary people who set out to get extraordinary results.

Millionaires come from such varied fields as retailing, computers, medicine, farming, garbage disposal, entertainment, real estate, manufacturing, and finance.

Some people still believe that luck determines one's financial destiny. I hope you learn to *detest* the word "luck." Your chances of lucking into wealth are too remote to calculate. Yet, millions of people put their faith in luck every day. Recently, after I told an audience that nine people become millionaires every hour, one fellow said to me (and he was serious), "I didn't know we had that many lotteries."

And other people are convinced the only way to become wealthy is in the "visible" organizations, professional sports, acting, and creative pursuits. Wrong! More than 99 percent of actors, artists, and writers must work outside these professions just to make a living. And only one athlete in 12,000 who plays football in high school will be offered a contract with a pro team.

Often people ask, "How is wealth divided?" According to official government statistics, wealth is divided almost the same today as it was 40 years ago.

Here are five keys to wealth and lasting prosperity:
- Make a complete commitment to wealth accumulation.
- Pay your financial freedom tax.
- Take charge of your economy.
- Avoid dumb debt; use smart debt instead.
- Participate in the coming Golden Age.

KEY 1: MAKE A COMPLETE COMMITMENT TO WEALTH ACCUMULATION

It's often said three things determine the value of real estate: Location, location, and location. What will make your wealth accumulation plan succeed? Again, three things: commitment, commitment, and commitment.

There are many ways to invest your money to accumulate wealth.

Real estate provides excellent money-building opportunities — raw land, investment property, rental units, housing projects, and more. Common stocks, mutual funds, your own business, preferred stock, bonds, oil well ventures are still other potentially excellent ways to use some of your money to acquire wealth.

Now here is a concept you must grasp to become financially independent: *Your commitment to your wealth plan is more important than your investment strategy.* It is much easier to find a way to invest your money than to apply the self-discipline required to make the strategy work. More people fail to accumulate wealth because they lack commitment to a plan than fail because their investment strategy is faulty. It boils down to this: Your attitude — your level of commitment — is the key in your wealth accumulation. The best investment strategy on earth won't work unless you *want* to make it work and are committed to making it work through persistent application.

Commitment comes from self-discipline. Discipline demands an automatic, systematic will to achieve goals. Unfortunately, few people can exercise self-discipline because they are not trained in the home, school, or on the job to practice it. An authority figure has always provided substitute discipline for them.

Self-discipline by definition is self-imposed and self-directed. Early in life, our parents tell us what to do and how to do it. When our behavior doesn't meet our parents' standards, they correct it. Then we go to school and teachers make us do certain things and avoid doing others so as to mold our behavior. If we don't want to study the material (lack the self-discipline), the teacher tells us we must or risk a low grade or other penalty. If we don't want to run around the field one more time, the coach tells us we must if we want to make the team.

By the time most people finish school, they are so accustomed to being disciplined by others, they can't discipline themselves.

Many people can't even discipline themselves to report to work on time so the employer does it for them with a punch-in clock. For many years John Johnson, the amazingly successful entrepreneur who founded the magazine *Ebony*, would watch for employees who reported to work late or who lacked the self-discipline to dress appropriately.

Because self-discipline is often not taught in the home or school, many people go through life expecting other people to provide discipline for them. "Tell me what to do, how to do it, and when to do it" is the way a large score of the population elects to live. So people settle down to a life in which important decisions are dictated by someone else. They relied on the discipline imposed by the government through forced social security to provide for their old age.

The point: In wealth accumulation, you must generate your own discipline. You must demand of yourself, "I *will* invest. I will not let anything stop me. No personal crises or temptations will be strong enough to make me give up my wealth accumulation plan."

Seventy percent of people reaching age 65 are dependent on social security for their existence. These people lived their productive lives during the richest period in world history. Yet, they did not discipline themselves to create wealth for their senior years.

"I'll start investing when I get a raise." This promise rarely works. Even before the raise comes, most people have already been irresistibly tempted by something — a bigger apartment, a new car, more clothes, a "dream-filled" vacation. People who barely get by now and receive a ten percent pay increase will still barely get by six months later. Most people adjust their spending thermostats up to spend every dime of every pay increase. Because they lack self-discipline, the majority of people will always "barely get by."

The solution is to call upon all the self-discipline you have. *Invest even a higher percent of your income as it increases.* Enjoy the great satisfaction that is yours when you look at your net worth statement. Juggling your debts to "barely get by" won't make you happy.

"But I have so little to invest. It isn't worth fooling with." The amount you begin to invest is not nearly as important as getting the investment habit. Just as a tree farmer knows that little trees will become giants in time, the smart investor knows that a small amount invested consistently will, in time, make a fortune.

Consider the potential, the power of $1,000: One thousand dollars invested to appreciate at an average of 18 percent per year will be $32,000 in 20 years, $1,024,000 in 30 years, and $32,768,000 in 60 years! And a one-time investment of $10,000 that appreciates an average of 18 percent per year will be $320,000 in 20 years.

No allowance is made in these examples for taxes, but with good C.P.A. advice, they can be minimized. Nor is consideration given to inflation. Just keep in mind that well-selected investments over time greatly exceed inflation.

"But money corrupts people. I don't want wealth because it is bad for people." It's hard to believe this excuse for avoiding wealth creation is still made, but it is. Some still argue that wealth spoils people, destroys their values, causes family problems, leads to drugs, creates a climate for crime, and makes people cheat.

Morality is a complex problem. But don't blame wealth. Too much money is not the root of evil; too little money is. Blame poverty for most social problems. Consider these facts:

- The lower the income in a neighborhood, the higher the crime rate. Police across the nation spend 83 percent of their time in the seven percent poorest neighborhoods.
- The poorer the people, the greater the incidence of alcoholism and other forms of drug addiction. The poorest 20 percent of the people consumes three times as much alcohol as the richest 20 percent.
- Most prostitutes are poor. They work their trade to make money.
- Most human abuse, whether to child, to spouse, or to elderly parent, is tied to money problems.
- More domestic difficulties and divorces can be traced to money problems than to any other cause.

Here is something to think about. At this instant, more people are quarreling about money than about all other problems combined.

KEY 2: PAY YOUR FINANCIAL FREEDOM TAX. IT IS THE SEED OF RICHES

People who acquire wealth have the habit of investing a portion of everything they earn. Wealthy people get rich putting some of their money to work so it makes more money.

Here is a plan that will work and will help you build wealth just as surely as the sun rises. Enact your own Financial Freedom Tax (FFT). Whatever your income, tax yourself a certain percent. I recommend 15 percent with 10 percent as the absolute minimum. Impose this tax on your *gross* income, not on what you take home after deductions. Follow the example of the government. So, if your gross income is $2,000 per month, tax yourself $200. If it's $8,000 per month, put aside $800 for your wealth program. Then invest your FFT money for your future benefit. Regard it as your seed money to grow wealth. Capital is money used to make more money. Your FFT plan means you pay yourself.

Nobody likes paying taxes, but they do because the laws say you must. Now, apply the same discipline to yourself as the government exercises on you, and you will "find" the money to pay a tax that goes 100 percent to benefit you.

Here is a thought-stimulating observation about taxes. Do a street survey and ask people these questions:

"Last year, how much income tax did you pay?" Very likely, people will say, "I really don't know. I think I'm in such and such a bracket, but I can't give you the exact amount."

Then ask how much they paid FICA (some taxpayers still don't know what it is). "How much did you pay in state income taxes? City income taxes? Sales taxes? Property taxes? Gasoline taxes? Taxes on airplane tickets?"

After you've interviewed the taxpayer, he or she will say something, such as "Look, I don't know how much tax I pay. All I know is I pay too much and I'm broke at the end of the month."

LOOK AT THESE ADVANTAGES OF TAXING YOURSELF

100 percent benefit to you. FFT is the only tax you will be glad to pay. One hundred percent of it goes for you and your family's benefit. None of your FFT goes to pay benefits to people who won't work or those who make welfare a career. And not a dime goes to pay tax collectors for the privilege of taking your money away to use for purposes you may not approve.

Also, if something happens to you before you decide to convert your invested FFT dollars to your own benefit, your estate will enjoy what you put aside. If you are single and pass away, all the money you were forced to pay into social security is gone. One hundred percent of your FFT goes to build a better life for you and your loved ones.

Under your complete control. You make all the decisions on how your FFT will be used. You may want to invest your money in mutual funds, a house or condo, land, bonds, or stocks. These and other investment vehicles are available to you. A savings account is a wonderful way to begin while you learn more about high-yielding-but-greater-risk ways to put your "tax" dollars to work.

Remember, you are not turning your FFT dollars over to the government to spend it the way the members of Congress choose to spend it — in a way to get themselves re-elected, i.e., for welfare to get votes, for aid to education to get votes, or for an unnecessarily large military establishment to get votes. Most members of Congress and the Senate have only one motive in mind — to get re-elected. So that's why they spend your money to hire more government employees and provide government services you don't want or need.

It costs nothing to collect. Think for a minute how much you must pay to the government for the privilege of paying the taxes it imposes — Federal government tax, state income taxes, state sales tax, property tax, capital gains tax. You are your own tax collector. So there's no waste there. The government often prides itself on how little it costs to take your money away from you. But the government does not tell people the truth. Your employer must employ people in the payroll department whose main job is to collect taxes. And if you're already self-employed, you are the government's tax collector. You spend your time or the time of your employees to collect money from yourself for the government to spend.

Source of enormous satisfaction. Your FFT helps you gain exactly what we call it — financial freedom. Collected regularly and invested carefully, your goal of financial freedom will be won. You can enjoy the goals you seek, the vacations, the visits to other lands, the food, and the housing you want, and you can help people the way you want to help them. Charity should not be run by the government.

Your FFT will create money. Your FFT will make your money grow more money. The IRS earns no money for you. The government can't even collect enough to break even. It has to borrow money just to pay its promises.

The taxes you pay the government are collected at one window and paid out at the next. But your FFT money goes to work for you and grows.

The reason the social security system stays in trouble is the money you pay into it is not invested to make more money. It's all paid out the same month you pay into it. Your FFT goes into your investments, compounds, and makes money for you. When you decide to cash in your FFT fund, there will be more in it than you "took" from yourself.

YOU CAN FIND THE MONEY TO PAY YOUR FFT!

Many people think, "I like the idea of an FFT, but there is nothing left over at the end of the month. I simply can't pay myself the FFT even if it all goes for me."

But you can! Suppose the government increased your income tax by 15 percent — something many government planners propose. Would you pay it? Of course. You don't want the IRS to sell your property. (Incidentally, the IRS is very much in the real estate business. In a typical year, it confiscates and sells tens of thousands of houses, buildings, lots, and farms to collect taxes people didn't pay on their properties.)

Or suppose the Social Security Administration decides to make even more people happy with the dole it hands out. So, it raises the amount you pay on your income from 7.5 percent to 8.5 percent. You think, "Well, that's only a penny on each dollar I earn. I can afford that." But that jump from 7.5 to 8.5 is actually an increase of about 12 percent! On a $35,000 income, that's $350. That $350 invested only once to compound at 18 percent would amount to $11,200 in 20 years and $358,400 in 40 years.

Or suppose you tell the person at the check-out stand, "Look, I don't like the sales tax. Please don't collect it on my food." The person will look at you as if to say, "What's wrong with this idiot?" and ring up the tax.

Or tell your employer, "I'm up against it right now. Had a bunch of unexpected bills. The kid got sick, the rent went up, and my car broke down. Please don't deduct any income tax this month." Your employer will simply say, "Sorry, it's the law. I have to withhold your income tax. Besides, the computer is already programmed to make the deduction."

Or tell the FICA tax representative, "I don't expect to collect social security for twenty (or thirty or forty) years. Please don't deduct any FICA on me for awhile." He'd say, "Pay or go to jail."

Get real stubborn and refuse to pay the property taxes on your house. It's only a matter of time until the tax people will sell your house and collect their taxes.

To reap the benefits of your hard work and pull yourself out of economic slavery, you must pay the FFT just as you pay the other taxes.

Remember, the FFT tax is the only tax you'll ever pay that goes to work for you and those you love. All other taxes are paid to people you don't know for purposes you may or may not approve.

The people who collect taxes for the IRS, FICA, city, state, or county may listen to your problems, but they will demand your money regardless.

So, before you do anything with your take-home pay, write a check to yourself first.

Like all steps to real financial success, the Financial Freedom Tax is simple but at first difficult to apply. The people who think, "I'm barely getting by now. I won't pay myself the FFT this month. I'll make it up next month" fool themselves.

The point: You will learn to adjust to your FFT. In three to six months, you won't miss the money you pay yourself for your sound economic future. Study the wealth accumulation steps that follow to see how you can and *will* invest part of what you earn for your benefit.

KEY 3: MAXIMIZE WHAT YOU EARN

Every year thousands of case histories reveal how some very big earners lose the money they worked hard to acquire. Joe Louis, perhaps the finest prize fighter of all time, was employed as a bouncer at a Las Vegas casino when he died. As a special tribute to a human "national treasure," Congress passed a special law to stop the Internal Revenue Service from trying to collect back taxes. Joe Louis simply couldn't pay what he owed the government.

It isn't unusual for one-time millionaire football players, screen actors, entertainers, and media personalities to become hopelessly in debt in their 40s or 50s.

"I'VE MADE $3.2 MILLION
AND MY NET WORTH IS $31,000"

Never equate income with wealth. Income is what you make. Wealth is what you own. A big income does not automatically make you wealthy.

Recently, I met a man in his late 40s who told me he had made over $3 million in his lifetime and has only $31,000 to show for it.

He explained, "I made a lot of money, but I made some lousy investments and went through two marriages. Then, twelve years ago I got into trouble with the IRS and they've been hounding me ever since."

I thought to myself, had this person paid himself the Financial Freedom Tax, he'd have quite a net worth statement today.

A friend who made $500,000 a year for a decade came to see me a month ago. "Sure, my family and I lived well while I was making big money. But I put all the surplus into the business. I didn't know until it was too late that my partner had been diverting company money to his own benefit. Now we have nothing. The bank is even foreclosing on our house."

Everyone earns a fortune in a lifetime. Yet, very few have a sizeable amount of wealth, if any, when they retire.

Consider this. We live in the richest, wealthiest nation on earth. Every citizen is guaranteed a free education. Everyone has equal opportunity. Yet during the last decade, more than 3,100,000 individuals went bankrupt! And more than half the people reaching age 65 are dependent on social security to live.

The point: Take action to manage your economy. Set aside 15 percent of what you earn to govern and compound, and you will stand up in any kind of economic storm.

THINK REWARD AND "SACRIFICE" WILL BE FUN

Wealth accumulation is the most challenging, exciting "game" you can play. Focus your energy and discipline on making money. Making money is not sacrifice. It simply is your way to achieve a worthwhile goal — financial freedom.

A young couple, Gail and Vic, told me of their first year's experience in launching their plan for financial independence. Gail explained, "We have two daughters, ages three and six, so I don't work. Vic makes a gross income of thirty-one thousand two hundred fifty dollars. We own a small home. And until a year ago, we spent every dime. But now we are on the road to wealth accumulation."

"What are you doing differently?" I asked.

"Well, Vic and I became unhappy with our financial circumstances. We were getting nowhere. So we decided to lay out a plan. We asked ourselves, 'Is a shiny new twelve thousand dollar car worth four times as much as a good three-year-old three thousand dollar car?' 'Whom do we impress?' 'For how long?' 'Do other people really care how new our cars are?'

'Will a two thousand dollar vacation buy us twice as much joy and satisfaction as a well-planned, closer-to-home, fewer-frills, one thousand dollar holiday?'

'Do we really need a second TV? What about life insurance?' We learned if it isn't term, we're simply telling the insurance company to get rich with our money.

"Vic and I went over every check we had written for a year. We literally took a look at every dollar we had spent."

"What other ways did you find to put aside more money for your financial freedom?" I asked.

"We found we subscribed to magazines we never read," Gail continued, "and we bought products only because they were on sale, purchased a lot of junk food, and, in other ways, let money slip through our fingers.

"So," Gail continued, "we looked for waste in our budget and found many big and little ways to save for investing. And we even found still other ideas to put money away to build wealth."

"Such as?" I asked.

"Smoking for one," Gail replied "Vic had been smoking two packs a day for years. I'd tell him smoking was bad for his health, but it did no good. Now, when Vic realized he was spending seventy-five dollars a month which, if compounded at twelve percent over the next thirty-two years — that's when he'll be sixty-five — would total close to a half-million dollars, he quit!" (Gail's comment made me recall that, grouped together, Americans spend five percent of their income on tobacco and alcohol annually. That's 50 percent of the minimum investment goal of 10 percent we've established for the financial freedom tax.)

"Well," I commented, "it's obvious you've given much thought to spending and budgeting. How have you translated your attitude into investing?"

"We've really planned. In our first year of wealth accumulation, we put forty-six hundred dollars away into growth mutual funds. And that's in addition to Vic's IRA."

"Tell me," I asked, "was it really a big sacrifice?"

Gail thought a moment. Then said, seriously, "It was no sacrifice at all. We simply are living a lot smarter. And it's fun, too. Now we feel like we're getting somewhere."

KEY 4: USE SMART DEBT AND AVOID DUMB DEBT

Smart debt is money you borrow to make more money. When you borrow money at, say, 10 percent with a good plan for getting a 15, 20 or 25 percent return on that money, you are a smart debtor. Usually financing your home and other real estate with a long-term mortgage is smart debt.

Dumb debt is borrowing money on credit cards and using installment pay plans to finance a car, appliances, or furniture. When you borrow money for vacations, entertainment, clothing, and a big splurge, you are a dumb debtor. The interest rate you pay is at least 50 percent higher than the basic cost of money — the prime rate. And you are subtracting from your future income.

Recently, I observed a 28-year-old single woman open her mail. She shouted with glee, "I got it! I got it!"

"You got what?" I asked, wondering what made my friend so happy.

"My American Express card! It has arrived! Look at it. Now I'm one of the chosen few. I can buy on credit almost everywhere."

I could understand my young friend's reaction. People crave status. People want to own things that not everyone can have. To this woman, the American Express card said, "You have a job, make a decent living, you have a good credit rating. You are now considered worthy of trust in the financial community."

But then I asked myself, "Is the credit card a blessing or a curse? Will it help or hinder the young lady gain wealth?"

My mind turned to other things that were once status symbols like cigarettes. Before the health facts of smoking were known, promoters of cigarettes promised smoking made people attractive, desirable, appealing. The manufacturer of Camels promised people that cigarettes steadied their nerves and aided digestion. The ads showed people saying, "I'd walk a mile for a Camel." Now, some of the people who started smoking Camels then can't even walk a block for anything! The emphysema, cancer, heart disease, and generally bad health caused by smoking is the large price smokers pay for what they thought was status.

Alcohol is sold for its power to make you a person of "distinction" and "sophistication" and one "to be admired" as a "role model."

A credit card is an economic gun many people use to kill future prosperity. It's like a drug to an addict. The card brings immediate euphoria only to be followed by discomfort of the worst sort.

If we had a "financial general" like we have a "surgeon general," he or she would put this notice on every credit card: "Warning. Use of this card is dangerous to your financial health. It may lead to overspending, financial problems, and financial death (bankruptcy)."

Everyone knows what's good about a credit card. It's convenient, widely accepted, and we don't have to carry a lot of cash and risk being robbed. And it provides a record of how much we spend, when and where. Credit cards are indispensable in business.

But the negative side of credit cards can interfere with your wealth accumulation program. Here's why. The card costs you an annual service fee. The interest rate that credit card companies charge you is about double the going price of money. And worst of all, a credit card promotes excessive and wasteful spending. "Buy now, pay later" is an attractive temptation many people can't resist. Restaurant managers like credit card customers because, on the average, the plastic customers spend 40 percent more than cash customers and they leave bigger tips.

The wisdom of the biblical quotation "You reap what you sow" applies to credit. You pay dearly for your debts. Credit is never free. It always costs.

Credit cards encourage people to waste money. That plastic card helps you to lose caution, gives you a false sense of security, and makes you think, "I'll figure out how to pay later." A misused credit card helps you dig your economic grave.

So, use credit cards only for the right reasons. Never use them because you don't have money in your checking account. Remember, every month about 300,000 cards are cancelled by credit card companies because the cardholders can't pay.

There are many sayings in our culture that tell you to spend every cent you can right now. "Live fast, die young, and have a beautiful corpse." "Eat, drink, and be merry, for tomorrow you may die." "Live for today," and "Whatever will be, will be" are short-term prescriptions for happiness.

Isn't it wiser to take a longer, positive, constructive approach to living?

THINK MICRO-ECONOMICS.
THINK, "WHAT IS BEST FOR ME?"

For decades, I have had an ongoing deep relationship with a super-millionaire. Now aged 87, his net worth exceeds $400 million. Despite his enormous wealth, his life style is extraordinarily simple — no yacht, no private planes, one live-in maid. His main economic goal is making money "because I enjoy it, and the more money I make, the more good I can do for others." He is generous for good causes and helps a lot of people, mostly anonymously.

My wealthy friend came from a poor family, so he acquired his vast wealth starting from nothing. But he often tells me, "My parents taught me religious principles. And I have found more good money-making ideas in the Bible than in all the other books I've read."

My friend and I have spent many hours together discussing the mystery of wealth accumulation. Here is one bit of advice that is applicable today: "You know," he said, "I was forty-five years old before I knew what the words micro- and macro-economics meant. But when I learned what they meant, I understood why I was doing so well. I had been practicing micro-economics all my life without knowing it. You see, most people read the headlines. They listen to business news every day. They think day-to-day fluctuations are important. To me, they are not. People think their personal economic future is tied to the national picture. If the economy is going into a recession, they assume their personal finances are going to slide, too. Or if the economy goes into a boom, they think they're going to benefit.

"Now this is foolish," my friend continued, "I don't worry about the American economy, the European economy, or the world economy. I am concerned with *my* economy. I've never paid much attention to the Dow Jones stock averages. I look at the logic of each situation. Logic told me back in the fifties that the second half of the Twentieth Century belonged to the South and Southern California. So I invested in real estate in Atlanta, Dallas, and San Diego. I traveled a lot in those days and I could tell some big northern cities had real problems.

"You see," he continued, "good people make money regardless of the economy. And fools will lose their money in the best of times. Just because other people are financially sick doesn't mean you've got to get sick, too. Even the worst epidemic kills only a fraction of the people. Same is true of a recession. Most businesses survive and the best ones are always better off."

"What about gold?" I asked.

"Well," my friend answered. "I sure can't tell you how much gold will bring next year or even in five years. But I do know this. Over the long pull, we've always had inflation, and the price of gold goes up with cheap money. I remember reading where we gave the Indians twenty-five dollars' worth of beads for Manhattan. The way I figure it, the Indians got a good deal. Had I invested twenty-five dollars in sixteen twenty-six when we bought the island and made only fifteen percent compounded, I'd have more now than the whole island is worth.

"You asked about gold — well, when Roosevelt took us off the gold standard, it was fixed at thirty-five dollars an ounce. When inflation hits us again real hard, gold will shoot way up."

"You're saying inflation will continue?" I asked.

"Oh yes!" he explained, "it's inevitable. But it always comes in spurts. It's never steady like five or eleven percent per year. During some periods there will be little or none — maybe even deflation. But every decade or so, there will be a big jump. But inflation doesn't bother me. Good investments will almost always increase in value more than the rate of inflation. Before I invest in anything I always get at least two, sometimes three or four, opinions. I listen. But I always make up my own mind. I figure it's my money and no one is as interested as I am in doing what's right."

The point: Think micro-economics. Think what's best for you. Never do anything — especially invest money — simply because other people are. Get advice, but make up your own mind.

KEY 5: PARTICIPATE IN THE COMING GOLDEN AGE

All times are filled with opportunity. But never has the future promised so much for so many. We are poised on the launch pad of a truly Golden Age. The world is like a bunch of horses ready for a thrilling, rewarding, exciting race. Here is why.

World-wide economic integration. Nations are becoming increasingly economically interdependent. Increased world trade in goods and services means nations because of their skills, climate, technology, or resources can advantageously specialize in producing products. One important result of world economic integration will be greatly increased productivity — more good things for people to enjoy.

Another benefit of growing economic interdependency is a decrease in the chance for war. Just as people who need each other are not inclined to fight, nations that depend on each other will not go to war.

Population growth will continue. The main fuel for the enormous economic expansion following World War II was population growth. During the period 1945-1985, the United States population grew by 100 million. More people translated into more houses, schools, churches, roads, books, recreation, medical care — all the products people need because they are people.

Some people feel population growth is wrong. Pessimists, defeatists, and faultfinders say the United States (and the world) is already overpopulated. According to them, we are running out of space, water, food, air, and other ingredients necessary to good living.

Don't let the petty negative thinkers pollute your mind. The United States will have no problem supporting a population of 400 million to 500 million people (roughly double its current size) in three or four decades.

Consider these facts:

- Despite a growth in population from 90 million in 1885

to 240 million in 1985, fewer acres were farmed and people were far better clothed, fed, and sheltered. Hunger that may exist today is a political problem, not a production, economic, or technological problem.

- There are more than ten acres of land (425,000 square feet) for every man, woman, and child in the U.S.A.
- If people live in overcrowded conditions (New York City, Washington, D.C., or Chicago) it's because they want to, not because they have to.
- Seventy-five percent of the world's surface is covered by water. The technology is here to remove the salt and impurities if we need it.

Great opportunities exist for people who view population growth positively.

Technology will expand. Technology is already a major industry. But in terms of its potential, it is still an infant. Great opportunities for careers, businesses, and investments are increasing fast in such fields as genetic engineering, solar and wind energy, disease eradication and prevention, and deep space exploitation. Technology will enable us to build an interstate highway system. Life expectancy may reach 95 years or longer. This and more in the decades immediately ahead — decades that impact directly on your future.

Human wants will still be insatiable. The concept Adam Smith gave us over two centuries ago that all human wants cannot be satisfied will be as true in the future as it is today. Consider travel — just one of dozens of opportunity areas. People cannot satisfy their desires to visit different parts of our nation and other nations. Only one American in 100 traveled outside the United States last year. And the more people travel, the more they want to travel. While international travel was at a record high last year, it is probable that it will increase at least five times in the next two decades. Think how the travel industry will affect other industries such as aircraft and hotels!

The Golden Age lies ahead. See it. Capitalize on it. Enjoy it. But remember. Just as people were blind to opportunity 40 years ago, most people will not discover the Golden Age until it is too late for them to benefit.

It is difficult to explain to a child how anyone can be poor today after the enormous economic growth and social betterment of the past 40 years. It will be even more difficult to explain personal mediocrity in the future.

Make your decision now to help shape up a wonderful future for yourself and those you love.

UNLOCK THESE KEYS TO PROSPERITY

- Make a complete commitment to wealth accumulation. The time to start is *now*, not when you get a raise, or when you have very little. Start now!
- Pay your financial freedom tax. Make paying "taxes" to yourself a passport to wealth.
- Maximize what you earn. Waste not, want not. Think to yourself that reward and sacrifice is fun.
- Use smart debt and avoid dumb debt.
- Think how you will survive, not how the economy will prosper.
- Participate in the coming Golden Age. The best is still to come.

A PERSONAL WORD FROM MELVIN POWERS
PUBLISHER, WILSHIRE BOOK COMPANY

Dear Friend:

My goal is to publish interesting, informative, and inspirational books. You can help me accomplish this by answering the following questions, either by phone or by mail. Or, if convenient for you, I would welcome the opportunity to visit with you in my office and hear your comments in person.

Did you enjoy reading this book? Why?

Would you enjoy reading another similar book?

What idea in the book impressed you the most?

If applicable to your situation, have you incorporated this idea in your daily life?

Is there a chapter that could serve as a theme for an entire book? Please explain.

If you have an idea for a book, I would welcome discussing it with you. If you already have one in progress, write or call me concerning possible publication. I can be reached at **(818) 765-8579.**

Sincerely yours,
MELVIN POWERS

12015 Sherman Road
North Hollywood, California 91605

MELVIN POWERS SELF-IMPROVEMENT LIBRARY

ASTROLOGY

____ ASTROLOGY: HOW TO CHART YOUR HOROSCOPE *Max Heindel*	5.00
____ ASTROLOGY AND SEXUAL ANALYSIS *Morris C. Goodman*	5.00
____ ASTROLOGY AND YOU *Carroll Righter*	5.00
____ ASTROLOGY MADE EASY *Astarte*	5.00
____ ASTROLOGY, ROMANCE, YOU AND THE STARS *Anthony Norvell*	5.00
____ MY WORLD OF ASTROLOGY *Sydney Omarr*	7.00
____ THOUGHT DIAL *Sydney Omarr*	7.00
____ WHAT THE STARS REVEAL ABOUT THE MEN IN YOUR LIFE *Thelma White*	3.00

BRIDGE

____ BRIDGE BIDDING MADE EASY *Edwin B. Kantar*	10.00
____ BRIDGE CONVENTIONS *Edwin B. Kantar*	7.00
____ COMPETITIVE BIDDING IN MODERN BRIDGE *Edgar Kaplan*	7.00
____ DEFENSIVE BRIDGE PLAY COMPLETE *Edwin B. Kantar*	15.00
____ GAMESMAN BRIDGE—PLAY BETTER WITH KANTAR *Edwin B. Kantar*	5.00
____ HOW TO IMPROVE YOUR BRIDGE *Alfred Sheinwold*	5.00
____ IMPROVING YOUR BIDDING SKILLS *Edwin B. Kantar*	4.00
____ INTRODUCTION TO DECLARER'S PLAY *Edwin B. Kantar*	7.00
____ INTRODUCTION TO DEFENDER'S PLAY *Edwin B. Kantar*	7.00
____ KANTAR FOR THE DEFENSE *Edwin B. Kantar*	7.00
____ KANTAR FOR THE DEFENSE VOLUME 2 *Edwin B. Kantar*	7.00
____ TEST YOUR BRIDGE PLAY *Edwin B. Kantar*	5.00
____ VOLUME 2—TEST YOUR BRIDGE PLAY *Edwin B. Kantar*	7.00
____ WINNING DECLARER PLAY *Dorothy Hayden Truscott*	7.00

BUSINESS, STUDY & REFERENCE

____ BRAINSTORMING *Charles Clark*	7.00
____ CONVERSATION MADE EASY *Elliot Russell*	4.00
____ EXAM SECRET *Dennis B. Jackson*	3.00
____ FIX-IT BOOK *Arthur Symons*	2.00
____ HOW TO DEVELOP A BETTER SPEAKING VOICE *M. Hellier*	4.00
____ HOW TO SELF-PUBLISH YOUR BOOK & MAKE IT A BEST SELLER *Melvin Powers*	10.00
____ INCREASE YOUR LEARNING POWER *Geoffrey A. Dudley*	3.00
____ PRACTICAL GUIDE TO BETTER CONCENTRATION *Melvin Powers*	3.00
____ PRACTICAL GUIDE TO PUBLIC SPEAKING *Maurice Forley*	5.00
____ 7 DAYS TO FASTER READING *William S. Schaill*	5.00
____ SONGWRITERS' RHYMING DICTIONARY *Jane Shaw Whitfield*	7.00
____ SPELLING MADE EASY *Lester D. Basch & Dr. Milton Finkelstein*	3.00
____ STUDENT'S GUIDE TO BETTER GRADES *J. A. Rickard*	3.00
____ TEST YOURSELF—FIND YOUR HIDDEN TALENT *Jack Shafer*	3.00
____ YOUR WILL & WHAT TO DO ABOUT IT *Attorney Samuel G. Kling*	5.00

CALLIGRAPHY

____ ADVANCED CALLIGRAPHY *Katherine Jeffares*	7.00
____ CALLIGRAPHER'S REFERENCE BOOK *Anne Leptich & Jacque Evans*	7.00
____ CALLIGRAPHY—THE ART OF BEAUTIFUL WRITING *Katherine Jeffares*	7.00
____ CALLIGRAPHY FOR FUN & PROFIT *Anne Leptich & Jacque Evans*	7.00
____ CALLIGRAPHY MADE EASY *Tina Serafini*	7.00

CHESS & CHECKERS

____ BEGINNER'S GUIDE TO WINNING CHESS *Fred Reinfeld*	5.00
____ CHESS IN TEN EASY LESSONS *Larry Evans*	5.00
____ CHESS MADE EASY *Milton L. Hanauer*	5.00
____ CHESS PROBLEMS FOR BEGINNERS *Edited by Fred Reinfeld*	5.00
____ CHESS TACTICS FOR BEGINNERS *Edited by Fred Reinfeld*	5.00
____ CHESS THEORY & PRACTICE *Morry & Mitchell*	2.00
____ HOW TO WIN AT CHECKERS *Fred Reinfeld*	5.00

____	1001 BRILLIANT WAYS TO CHECKMATE *Fred Reinfeld*	7.00
____	1001 WINNING CHESS SACRIFICES & COMBINATIONS *Fred Reinfeld*	7.00

COOKERY & HERBS

____	CULPEPER'S HERBAL REMEDIES *Dr. Nicholas Culpeper*	3.00
____	FAST GOURMET COOKBOOK *Poppy Cannon*	2.50
____	GINSENG—THE MYTH & THE TRUTH *Joseph P. Hou*	3.00
____	HEALING POWER OF HERBS *May Bethel*	5.00
____	HEALING POWER OF NATURAL FOODS *May Bethel*	5.00
____	HERBS FOR HEALTH—HOW TO GROW & USE THEM *Louise Evans Doole*	4.00
____	HOME GARDEN COOKBOOK—DELICIOUS NATURAL FOOD RECIPES *Ken Kraft*	3.00
____	MEDICAL HERBALIST *Edited by Dr. J. R. Yemm*	3.00
____	VEGETABLE GARDENING FOR BEGINNERS *Hugh Wiberg*	2.00
____	VEGETABLES FOR TODAY'S GARDENS *R. Milton Carleton*	2.00
____	VEGETARIAN COOKERY *Janet Walker*	7.00
____	VEGETARIAN COOKING MADE EASY & DELECTABLE *Veronica Vezza*	3.00
____	VEGETARIAN DELIGHTS—A HAPPY COOKBOOK FOR HEALTH *K. R. Mehta*	2.00
____	VEGETARIAN GOURMET COOKBOOK *Joyce McKinnel*	3.00

GAMBLING & POKER

____	ADVANCED POKER STRATEGY & WINNING PLAY *A. D. Livingston*	5.00
____	HOW TO WIN AT DICE GAMES *Skip Frey*	3.00
____	HOW TO WIN AT POKER *Terence Reese & Anthony T. Watkins*	5.00
____	WINNING AT CRAPS *Dr. Lloyd T. Commins*	5.00
____	WINNING AT GIN *Chester Wander & Cy Rice*	3.00
____	WINNING AT POKER—AN EXPERT'S GUIDE *John Archer*	5.00
____	WINNING AT 21—AN EXPERT'S GUIDE *John Archer*	5.00
____	WINNING POKER SYSTEMS *Norman Zadeh*	3.00

HEALTH

____	BEE POLLEN *Lynda Lyngheim & Jack Scagnetti*	3.00
____	COPING WITH ALZHEIMER'S *Rose Oliver, Ph.D. & Francis Bock, Ph.D.*	7.00
____	DR. LINDNER'S SPECIAL WEIGHT CONTROL METHOD *Peter G. Lindner, M.D.*	2.00
____	HELP YOURSELF TO BETTER SIGHT *Margaret Darst Corbett*	3.00
____	HOW YOU CAN STOP SMOKING PERMANENTLY *Ernest Caldwell*	5.00
____	MIND OVER PLATTER *Peter G. Lindner, M.D.*	3.00
____	NATURE'S WAY TO NUTRITION & VIBRANT HEALTH *Robert J. Scrutton*	3.00
____	NEW CARBOHYDRATE DIET COUNTER *Patti Lopez-Pereira*	2.00
____	REFLEXOLOGY *Dr. Maybelle Segal*	4.00
____	REFLEXOLOGY FOR GOOD HEALTH *Anna Kaye & Don C. Matchan*	5.00
____	30 DAYS TO BEAUTIFUL LEGS *Dr. Marc Selner*	3.00
____	YOU CAN LEARN TO RELAX *Dr. Samuel Gutwirth*	3.00
____	YOUR ALLERGY—WHAT TO DO ABOUT IT *Allan Knight, M.D.*	3.00

HOBBIES

____	BEACHCOMBING FOR BEGINNERS *Norman Hickin*	2.00
____	BLACKSTONE'S MODERN CARD TRICKS *Harry Blackstone*	5.00
____	BLACKSTONE'S SECRETS OF MAGIC *Harry Blackstone*	5.00
____	COIN COLLECTING FOR BEGINNERS *Burton Hobson & Fred Reinfeld*	5.00
____	ENTERTAINING WITH ESP *Tony 'Doc' Shiels*	2.00
____	400 FASCINATING MAGIC TRICKS YOU CAN DO *Howard Thurston*	5.00
____	HOW I TURN JUNK INTO FUN AND PROFIT *Sari*	3.00
____	HOW TO WRITE A HIT SONG & SELL IT *Tommy Boyce*	7.00
____	JUGGLING MADE EASY *Rudolf Dittrich*	3.00
____	MAGIC FOR ALL AGES *Walter Gibson*	4.00
____	MAGIC MADE EASY *Byron Wels*	2.00
____	STAMP COLLECTING FOR BEGINNERS *Burton Hobson*	3.00

HORSE PLAYER'S WINNING GUIDES

____	BETTING HORSES TO WIN *Les Conklin*	5.00
____	ELIMINATE THE LOSERS *Bob McKnight*	5.00

MARRIAGE, SEX & PARENTHOOD

_____ ABILITY TO LOVE *Dr. Allan Fromme*	7.00
_____ GUIDE TO SUCCESSFUL MARRIAGE *Drs. Albert Ellis & Robert Harper*	7.00
_____ HOW TO RAISE AN EMOTIONALLY HEALTHY, HAPPY CHILD *Albert Ellis, Ph.D.*	7.00
_____ PARENT SURVIVAL TRAINING *Marvin Silverman, Ed.D. & David Lustig, Ph.D.*	10.00
_____ SEX WITHOUT GUILT *Albert Ellis, Ph.D.*	5.00
_____ SEXUALLY ADEQUATE MALE *Frank S. Caprio, M.D.*	3.00
_____ SEXUALLY FULFILLED MAN *Dr. Rachel Copelan*	5.00
_____ STAYING IN LOVE *Dr. Norton F. Kristy*	7.00

MELVIN POWERS' MAIL ORDER LIBRARY

_____ HOW TO GET RICH IN MAIL ORDER *Melvin Powers*	20.00
_____ HOW TO WRITE A GOOD ADVERTISEMENT *Victor O. Schwab*	20.00
_____ MAIL ORDER MADE EASY *J. Frank Brumbaugh*	20.00

METAPHYSICS & OCCULT

_____ BOOK OF TALISMANS, AMULETS & ZODIACAL GEMS *William Pavitt*	7.00
_____ CONCENTRATION—A GUIDE TO MENTAL MASTERY *Mouni Sadhu*	5.00
_____ EXTRA-TERRESTRIAL INTELLIGENCE—THE FIRST ENCOUNTER	6.00
_____ FORTUNE TELLING WITH CARDS *P. Foli*	5.00
_____ HOW TO INTERPRET DREAMS, OMENS & FORTUNE TELLING SIGNS *Gettings*	5.00
_____ HOW TO UNDERSTAND YOUR DREAMS *Geoffrey A. Dudley*	5.00
_____ IN DAYS OF GREAT PEACE *Mouni Sadhu*	3.00
_____ LSD—THE AGE OF MIND *Bernard Roseman*	2.00
_____ MAGICIAN—HIS TRAINING AND WORK *W. E. Butler*	5.00
_____ MEDITATION *Mouni Sadhu*	7.00
_____ MODERN NUMEROLOGY *Morris C. Goodman*	5.00
_____ NUMEROLOGY—ITS FACTS AND SECRETS *Ariel Yvon Taylor*	5.00
_____ NUMEROLOGY MADE EASY *W. Mykian*	5.00
_____ PALMISTRY MADE EASY *Fred Gettings*	5.00
_____ PALMISTRY MADE PRACTICAL *Elizabeth Daniels Squire*	5.00
_____ PALMISTRY SECRETS REVEALED *Henry Frith*	4.00
_____ PROPHECY IN OUR TIME *Martin Ebon*	2.50
_____ SUPERSTITION—ARE YOU SUPERSTITIOUS? *Eric Maple*	2.00
_____ TAROT *Mouni Sadhu*	10.00
_____ TAROT OF THE BOHEMIANS *Papus*	7.00
_____ WAYS TO SELF-REALIZATION *Mouni Sadhu*	7.00
_____ WITCHCRAFT, MAGIC & OCCULTISM—A FASCINATING HISTORY *W. B. Crow*	7.00
_____ WITCHCRAFT—THE SIXTH SENSE *Justine Glass*	7.00
_____ WORLD OF PSYCHIC RESEARCH *Hereward Carrington*	2.00

SELF-HELP & INSPIRATIONAL

_____ CHARISMA—HOW TO GET "THAT SPECIAL MAGIC" *Marcia Grad*	7.00
_____ DAILY POWER FOR JOYFUL LIVING *Dr. Donald Curtis*	5.00
_____ DYNAMIC THINKING *Melvin Powers*	5.00
_____ GREATEST POWER IN THE UNIVERSE *U. S. Andersen*	7.00
_____ GROW RICH WHILE YOU SLEEP *Ben Sweetland*	7.00
_____ GROWTH THROUGH REASON *Albert Ellis, Ph.D.*	7.00
_____ GUIDE TO PERSONAL HAPPINESS *Albert Ellis, Ph.D. & Irving Becker, Ed.D.*	7.00
_____ HANDWRITING ANALYSIS MADE EASY *John Marley*	5.00
_____ HANDWRITING TELLS *Nadya Olyanova*	7.00
_____ HOW TO ATTRACT GOOD LUCK *A.H.Z. Carr*	7.00
_____ HOW TO BE GREAT *Dr. Donald Curtis*	5.00
_____ HOW TO DEVELOP A WINNING PERSONALITY *Martin Panzer*	5.00
_____ HOW TO DEVELOP AN EXCEPTIONAL MEMORY *Young & Gibson*	5.00
_____ HOW TO LIVE WITH A NEUROTIC *Albert Ellis, Ph.D.*	7.00
_____ HOW TO OVERCOME YOUR FEARS *M. P. Leahy, M.D.*	3.00
_____ HOW TO SUCCEED *Brian Adams*	7.00
_____ HUMAN PROBLEMS & HOW TO SOLVE THEM *Dr. Donald Curtis*	5.00
_____ I CAN *Ben Sweetland*	7.00
_____ I WILL *Ben Sweetland*	3.00

___ KNIGHT IN THE RUSTY ARMOR *Robert Fisher*		5.00
___ LEFT-HANDED PEOPLE *Michael Barsley*		5.00
___ MAGIC IN YOUR MIND *U.S. Andersen*		7.00
___ MAGIC OF THINKING BIG *Dr. David J. Schwartz*		3.00
___ MAGIC OF THINKING SUCCESS *Dr. David J. Schwartz*		7.00
___ MAGIC POWER OF YOUR MIND *Walter M. Germain*		7.00
___ MENTAL POWER THROUGH SLEEP SUGGESTION *Melvin Powers*		3.00
___ NEVER UNDERESTIMATE THE SELLING POWER OF A WOMAN *Dottie Walters*		7.00
___ NEW GUIDE TO RATIONAL LIVING *Albert Ellis, Ph.D. & R. Harper, Ph.D.*		7.00
___ PSYCHO-CYBERNETICS *Maxwell Maltz, M.D.*		7.00
___ PSYCHOLOGY OF HANDWRITING *Nadya Olyanova*		7.00
___ SALES CYBERNETICS *Brian Adams*		7.00
___ SCIENCE OF MIND IN DAILY LIVING *Dr. Donald Curtis*		7.00
___ SECRET OF SECRETS *U.S. Andersen*		7.00
___ SECRET POWER OF THE PYRAMIDS *U. S. Andersen*		7.00
___ SELF-THERAPY FOR THE STUTTERER *Malcolm Frazer*		3.00
___ SUCCESS-CYBERNETICS *U. S. Andersen*		7.00
___ 10 DAYS TO A GREAT NEW LIFE *William E. Edwards*		3.00
___ THINK AND GROW RICH *Napoleon Hill*		7.00
___ THINK YOUR WAY TO SUCCESS *Dr. Lew Losoncy*		5.00
___ THREE MAGIC WORDS *U. S. Andersen*		7.00
___ TREASURY OF COMFORT *Edited by Rabbi Sidney Greenberg*		7.00
___ TREASURY OF THE ART OF LIVING *Sidney S. Greenberg*		7.00
___ WHAT YOUR HANDWRITING REVEALS *Albert E. Hughes*		3.00
___ YOUR SUBCONSCIOUS POWER *Charles M. Simmons*		7.00
___ YOUR THOUGHTS CAN CHANGE YOUR LIFE *Dr. Donald Curtis*		7.00

SPORTS

___ BICYCLING FOR FUN AND GOOD HEALTH *Kenneth E. Luther*		2.00
___ BILLIARDS—POCKET • CAROM • THREE CUSION *Clive Cottingham, Jr.*		5.00
___ COMPLETE GUIDE TO FISHING *Vlad Evanoff*		2.00
___ HOW TO IMPROVE YOUR RACQUETBALL *Lubarsky, Kaufman & Scagnetti*		5.00
___ HOW TO WIN AT POCKET BILLIARDS *Edward D. Knuchell*		7.00
___ JOY OF WALKING *Jack Scagnetti*		3.00
___ LEARNING & TEACHING SOCCER SKILLS *Eric Worthington*		3.00
___ MOTORCYCLING FOR BEGINNERS *I.G. Edmonds*		3.00
___ RACQUETBALL FOR WOMEN *Toni Hudson, Jack Scagnetti & Vince Rondone*		3.00
___ RACQUETBALL MADE EASY *Steve Lubarsky, Rod Delson & Jack Scagnetti*		5.00
___ SECRET OF BOWLING STRIKES *Dawson Taylor*		5.00
___ SECRET OF PERFECT PUTTING *Horton Smith & Dawson Taylor*		5.00
___ SOCCER—THE GAME & HOW TO PLAY IT *Gary Rosenthal*		5.00
___ STARTING SOCCER *Edward F. Dolan, Jr.*		5.00

TENNIS LOVER'S LIBRARY

___ BEGINNER'S GUIDE TO WINNING TENNIS *Helen Hull Jacobs*		2.00
___ HOW TO BEAT BETTER TENNIS PLAYERS *Loring Fiske*		4.00
___ HOW TO IMPROVE YOUR TENNIS—STYLE, STRATEGY & ANALYSIS *C. Wilson*		2.00
___ PSYCH YOURSELF TO BETTER TENNIS *Dr. Walter A. Luszki*		2.00
___ TENNIS FOR BEGINNERS *Dr. H. A. Murray*		2.00
___ TENNIS MADE EASY *Joel Brecheen*		5.00
___ WEEKEND TENNIS—HOW TO HAVE FUN & WIN AT THE SAME TIME *Bill Talbert*		3.00
___ WINNING WITH PERCENTAGE TENNIS—SMART STRATEGY *Jack Lowe*		2.00

WILSHIRE PET LIBRARY

___ DOG OBEDIENCE TRAINING *Gust Kessopulos*		5.00
___ DOG TRAINING MADE EASY & FUN *John W. Kellogg*		5.00
___ HOW TO BRING UP YOUR PET DOG *Kurt Unkelbach*		2.00
___ HOW TO RAISE & TRAIN YOUR PUPPY *Jeff Griffen*		5.00

The books listed above can be obtained from your book dealer or directly from Melvin Powers. When ordering, please remit $1.50 postage for the first book and 50¢ for each additional book.

Melvin Powers
12015 Sherman Road, No. Hollywood, California 91605

WILSHIRE HORSE LOVERS' LIBRARY

The books listed above can be obtained from your book dealer or directly from Melvin Powers. When ordering, please remit $1.50 postage for the first book and 50¢ for each additional book.

Melvin Powers

12015 Sherman Road, No. Hollywood, California 91605